WINNING TIPS FOR CASINO GAMES

John Grochowski

Publications International, Ltd.

John Grochowski writes about playing casino games and the gambling industry in his weekly *Gaming* column for the *Chicago Sun-Times*. His column is syndicated nationally by the Chicago Sun-Times Features Syndicate and his stories and articles on gambling have appeared in magazines including *Casino, Casino Player,* and *Casino Executive.*

CONTENTS

AMERICA'S FASTEST-GROWING PASTIME

For generations of Americans, casino gambling meant Las Vegas—and the name evoked either glamour or tacky glitz, depending on the listener. In addition, a backdrop of underworld ties made the nation's gambling capital a place many were wary of visiting. But in the '90s, the limits are off. Corporate ownership of casinos and huge themed resorts designed to attract whole families have given Las Vegas a clean image.

Today, almost everywhere you look across the United States, it seems casinos are dotting the landscape. Casino gambling has been established in Atlantic City since 1978. In addition to the land-based casinos of Nevada and New Jersey, riverboat casinos have opened in Illinois, Iowa, Louisiana, Mississippi, and Missouri, with Indiana boats scheduled for 1995 openings. Low-limit land-based casinos are in Colorado and South Dakota, and New Orleans has one large full-service land-based casino. And Native American tribes bring casino gambling to much of the rest of the country. Tribal casinos or bingo halls have opened in Arizona, California, Connecticut, Florida, Iowa, Louisiana, Massachusetts, Michigan, Minnesota, Mississippi, Montana, New Mexico, New York, North Carolina, North Dakota, Oregon, South Dakota, Washington, and Wisconsin.

A 1994 survey found that in the previous year, United States patrons made 92 million casino visits—twice the 1990 total of 46 million visits. More people visited casinos than attended major league baseball games or any other professional sporting events—than attended arena concerts—than attended Broadway shows. And that was before further expansion in 1994—the launching of the first Missouri gambling riverboats and new properties opening in established gambling markets. It seems casino gambling is becoming one of America's national pastimes.

Casino-goers come from all groups of the population—54 percent are women, 46 percent men; 54 percent have some college education; 50 percent have white-collar jobs, 26 percent blue-collar; 24 percent are retired. The percentages of women and blue-collar workers are higher at newer gambling areas.

Can You Win?

Let's be realistic—casino gambling is best taken as a form of entertainment. In the long run, the casinos will be the winners—those resort hotels and riverboats aren't built to drive themselves out of business by giving money away to the players.

Except for blackjack, which has odds that change continuously as cards are dealt out, casino games are designed with a fixed mathematical edge in favor of the house. In roulette, for instance, the wheel has 38 numbers—1 though 36, plus 0 and 00. To use the simplest example, the player may place a bet on any one of those 38 numbers. A winning bet will bring a payoff of 35-1—the player gets his original bet back, plus 35 times the bet in winnings. If there were no 0 or 00, that would correspond exactly to the odds of winning, but with those numbers added, the true odds are 37-1. By paying at less than the true odds, the house builds in a 5.26 percent advantage in roulette.

Does that mean it's hopeless for the player, that the house will win every time? No, for if there were no winners, there soon would be no customers. In the long run, the percentage will hold up and the casino will make its profit. But in the short term, results vary widely from the norm. The house advantages in casino games are narrow enough to produce winners—lots of winners, in fact—every day.

For the best chance to win—and to limit losses—players need to understand the games

HOUSE PERCENTAGES

Casino advantages in the major games offered stack up this way:

Blackjack	0 to 1 percent (basic strategy player)	2 to 5 percent (average player)
Craps	0.6 percent (pass/come with double odds)	16.67 percent (the worst proposition bets)
Baccarat/Mini-baccarat	1.17 percent (bet on banker)	1.36 percent (bet on player)
Roulette	5.26 percent on all bets but the five-number bet on 0, 00, 1, 2, and 3, which carries a 7.89-percent house edge	
Slot machines	Varies according to programming; average is about 5 or 6 percent on $1 machines or 8 to 10 percent on 25-cent machines	
Jacks or Better video poker	0.4 percent with optimal play on a full-pay 9-6 machine	3.8 percent on a 7-5 machine

before they start to play. A blackjack player who does not know the rules of the game, the totals on which the dealer is required to hit or stand, or a basic strategy for play might as well just write the casino a check. Likewise, a craps player who does not understand the available options might make bets giving the house a 16.67 percent edge, when bets are available at the same table that limit the house advantage to .6 percent.

Use this book as a guide to each casino game. Learn the best bets and stay away from the worst ones, and you'll win more often. But understand that regardless of how well you play, sometimes—the majority of times, in fact—the house edge is going to grind down your bankroll.

First-Time Basics

If your vision of casino players is James Bond, in a tux, at Monte Carlo, forget it. American casinos do not enforce that kind of formality. Casual clothing and sportswear are most common, but you'll see everything from evening wear to T-shirts and jeans in the same casino.

Many casinos give free beverages to players. In some states it's illegal to give free alcoholic beverages to casino customers, so casinos in these jurisdictions charge for alcohol but usually give free soft drinks and coffee to playing customers. In either case, it's appropriate to tip the cocktail server—a couple of quarters or a dollar will do.

Be sure you know the bet requirements at a particular slot machine or table game before you sit down. On slots or video poker, the denomination is either painted on the machine's glass or displayed on a video screen.

It won't cost you anything to put a quarter in a dollar machine—the smaller quarter will drop right through without activating anything—and you won't be able to fit a dollar token into a quarter slot.

At table games, each table has a rectangular sign detailing minimum and maximum bets. Usually the signs are color-coded to correspond to the color of casino chips—a white sign usually denotes a table with a $1 minimum bet, a red sign denotes a $5 minimum, a green sign denotes a $25 minimum, and a black sign denotes a $100 minimum, just as at most casinos $1 chips are white, $5 chips are red, $25 chips are green, and $100 chips are black. Do not take this system for granted, however; a few casinos have signs all of the same color or use different color coding. Read the sign before sitting down to play.

Slot and video poker players will probably want to change currency for coins or tokens before going to a machine, though some newer machines are fitted with currency acceptors. Buy change either from a roving change person or from the change booth at the casino.

Table players change currency for casino chips at the tables. Place currency on the table layout and ask the dealer, "Change, please." The dealer will give you the corresponding amount in chips and will push your money into a locked drop box.

CASINO "COMPS"

Casinos want to keep their best customers coming back. Players who have shown they will give the house a shot at their money are treated like royalty. Free beverages for customers while they are playing, discounted rates on hotel rooms, and free meals are the most common complimentaries given by casinos. For high-rollers—people who bet hundreds of dollars a hand—the casino might give free airfare, room, food, beverages, or limousine service.

For slot machine and video poker players, "comps" are most frequently distributed through slot clubs. Members are issued credit-card-sized plastic cards, usually with an encoded magnetic strip on the back. The card is inserted into a magnetic reader on the machine the member is playing, and the amount and duration of play are tracked via computer.

In some slot clubs, players earn points for play and can redeem the points for comps. When the card is inserted, a display on the reader might say something like, "Welcome, member. You have 42 points. Coins to next point: 24." After the required number of coins have been played, another point will be added to the player's total. A list is issued detailing the comps available for various point totals. Some clubs allow players to redeem points for cash; others offer meals, rooms, or merchandise.

Other slot clubs don't issue a point table but require the player to ask a slot host for the comps desired. The slot host will check the computer, and if the player qualifies, the host will issue the comp.

Comps work similarly at table games. At some casinos a player may use the same card issued to slot club members as identification to be rated for comps at table games. At others, the player must request a separate table rating. The pit boss overseeing the table takes note of the player's buy-in (the amount of currency exchanged for chips at the table), the average bet size, and the duration of play.

It's common for casinos to kick back in the form of comps an average of 20 percent to 40 percent of the amount it expects to win from the player.

The basic formula for the player's expected loss combines the amount of time played, the number of hands per hour, the average bet, and the house percentage. So if a blackjack player bets $5 a hand for an hour at a busy-table speed of 60 hands per hour, and the house figures it has a 2 percent edge, then the player is betting $300 per hour, and the house, on the average expects to win $6, or 2 percent of $300. If the house is issuing comps at a generous rate of 40 percent of the player's expected loss, the customer's play for an hour is worth about $2.40 in comps, regardless of the actual win or loss, whether he's won $50 or lost $50.

A side benefit of being rated for comps is that the casino puts you on its mailing list for special offers. Rated players frequently get free or discounted rooms and tournament invitations from casinos in resort areas. Riverboat casinos, many of which have admission charges, often waive those fees for rated players. They also issue invitations to special events.

When it comes time to leave, remember that the dealer does not have access to cash at the tables. To change your chips for cash, you must go to the casino cashier's booth. If you have a lot of smaller-denomination chips and wish to change for larger-denomination chips to make it easier to carry them to the cashier's booth, ask the dealer to "color up." He or she then will give you one green $25 chip for five red $5 chips, or a black $100 chip for twenty $5 chips, for example.

Slot players cash out by putting all their coins or tokens into one of the plastic coin cups provided by the casino, then taking the cup to the change booth. At the booth, an employee will run the change through a coin-counting machine, then give the corresponding amount of currency and coins to the customer. At some smaller casinos, the coin counters are located at the cashier's cage.

Payoffs

You'll sometimes find payoffs expressed in this book as "chances-TO-1"; other times, especially in video poker, they are expressed as "chances-FOR-1." In roulette, for example, the payoff for hitting a single number is 35-to-1. The player's one-unit bet stays on the table until the outcome is determined. If the player wins, he or she wins 35 units and gets to keep the original bet for a total of 36 units. But in video poker, the payoff for two pair is 2-for-1. The player has already put one unit down the slot and that is gone; the player who hits two pair gets a total of two units back for the one that has been wagered.

Bankroll

Do not go into a casino with money you can't afford to lose. Even at games with house percentages of less than 1 percent, there will be times the player just can't win. The worst thing a player can do is to start chasing losses, gambling money needed elsewhere in an attempt to win back money that's already gone.

Remember, the house percentage is in effect on every spin of the roulette wheel and every pull of the slot handle. No law of averages says you have to start winning just because you've been on a long losing streak. If you've been betting on "Even" in roulette and odd numbers have shown up ten times in a row, the next spin is no more or less likely to be an even number than any other spin. Each trial is independent, and the house advantage still is 5.26 percent. Treat your gambling bankroll as an entertainment expense and budget accordingly. Set limits on losses and stick to them.

Once you've decided how much to budget for the day, play at a level appropriate to your bankroll. If you have $20 for a two-hour riverboat cruise, you can't afford to play $1 slots or $5 blackjack. You'll need to stick to quarter slots, and at that you risk being finished for the day in about 15 minutes.

TIPPING DEALERS

The gambling business is a service industry, and dealers are paid like bottom-rung employees in service industries—not very well. Many dealers' jobs pay minimum wage, and the bulk of dealers' pay comes through tips from customers.

You are under no obligation to tip, and even the dealers don't expect you to tip while you're losing. However, if you are winning and the dealer is courteous and helpful, it's customary to tip. This can be done by simply pushing a chip forward onto the layout and telling the dealer, "This is for you." However, more frequently tips are given by placing a bet for the dealer.

In blackjack, the usual method for tipping is to place an additional bet at the front of your betting box. Don't tip so much or so frequently that you significantly shift the odds of the game. If you're betting $5 for yourself, a $1 bet for the dealer once or twice an hour, or when you're on a winning streak, will do. If you win the hand, the dealer will get a $2 tip. If you lose, the house gets the money.

Some older gambling guides tell of a cat-and-mouse game in which the blackjack player uses tips to get the dealer to deal another hand before shuffling when the cards remaining to be dealt are in the player's favor. This has little or no bearing on how the game is played today. In multiple-deck games dealt from a shoe, a colored plastic cut card is inserted into the shuffled cards to tell the dealer when to stop. When that cut card comes out, the dealer may not start another hand, regardless of what the player wants and how much he's willing to tip. Even in single- and double-deck games dealt from the hand, strict guidelines usually dictate when the dealer must shuffle. Sometimes a cut card is used. One Las Vegas casino simply shuffles on single-deck games every other hand, regardless of how many players are at the table. Don't tip with the expectation that the dealer will bend house rules on when to shuffle; tip for service with a smile.

Craps players also often place bets for the dealers. Most often, this is done either by telling a dealer to place a specific bet "for the boys"—bets on 11 or the field are among frequent choices—or by placing a bet on one of the "hard ways" and telling the dealer it goes both ways. That is, a $10 hard six both ways means the player is betting $5 for himself and $5 for the dealers that two threes will come up before a seven and before any other six. If you want to give the dealers the best chance to win, place a pass line bet for the boys. It's rarely done, and the crew will remember you.

Tips seem less frequent at the roulette wheel. Probably the most common is simply giving the dealer a chip after hitting a 35-1 single-number payoff. Don't hand it directly to the dealer—dealers are not allowed to take money or chips from a player's hand. Place it on the table and tell the dealer it's a tip.

Slot and video poker players are a solitary lot, and occasions for tipping are rare. However, if you hit a large, hand-paid jackpot, and service has been good from a change person, it doesn't hurt to tip.

In Illinois, where such statistics are released by the Illinois Gaming Board, the average casino customer loses about $40 on a typical riverboat cruise. But you need to bring more than that with you. You need enough of a cushion to ride out the inevitable losing streaks that happen in any game.

Here are some recommended minimum bankrolls for a two-hour casino stay:

25-cent slots and video poker	$100
$5-a-hand blackjack	$150
$5-per-spin roulette (even-money bets)	$100
$5 best-method craps (pass and two-come bets with double odds)	$500
$10-a-hand mini-baccarat (table minimums are usually higher than at other casino games)	$200

This is not to suggest that you should expect to lose $200 if you play mini-baccarat for a couple of hours. Your average outcome will be in the range of $10 to $20 in losses, and sometimes you'll walk away a winner.

An appropriate bankroll is a major part of winning more often and limiting losses the rest of the time.

SLOT MACHINES

In the not-too-distant past, slot-machine players were the second-class citizens of casino customers. Jackpots were small, payout percentages were horrendous, and slot players just weren't eligible for the kind of complimentary bonuses—free rooms, shows, meals— commonly given to table players. But in the last few decades the face of the casino industry has changed. Nowadays more than 60 percent of casino revenues comes from slot machines.

About 80 percent of first-time casino visitors head for the slots. It's easy—just drop coins into the slot and push the button or pull the handle. Newcomers can find the personal interaction with dealers or other players at the tables intimidating—slot players avoid that. And besides, the biggest, most lifestyle-changing jackpots in the casino are offered on the slots.

How to Play

The most popular slots come in 25-cent and $1 denominations, though there are penny, nickel, $5, $25, even $100 slot machines. Most take up to two or three coins at a time; a few take five coins or more.

In most casinos you go to a change person, the change booth, or the cashier's cage to change currency for coins or tokens to play in the machines. Many newer machines are fitted with currency acceptors—slide a bill into the slot, and the equivalent amount of credits is displayed on a meter. Drop the appropriate number of coins in the slot, then either pull the handle or push the button marked "Spin Reels." If playing against credits, you can push a button marked "Play One Credit" until you've reached the number of coins you wish to play, then hit the spin button or pull the handle. Or you can hit a button marked "Play Max Credits," which will play the maximum coins allowed on that machine and spin the reels.

Many machines have a single payout line painted across the center of the glass in front of the reels. Others have three payout lines, even five payout lines, each corresponding to a coin played. The symbols that stop on a payout line determine whether a player wins. A common set of symbols might be cherries, bars, double bars (two bars stacked atop one another), triple bars, and sevens. A single cherry on the payout line, for example, might pay back two coins; the player might get 10 coins for three of any bars (a mixture of bars, double bars, and triple bars), 30 for three single bars, 60 for three double bars, 120 for three triple bars, and the jackpot for three sevens. However, many of the stops on each reel will be blanks, and a combination that

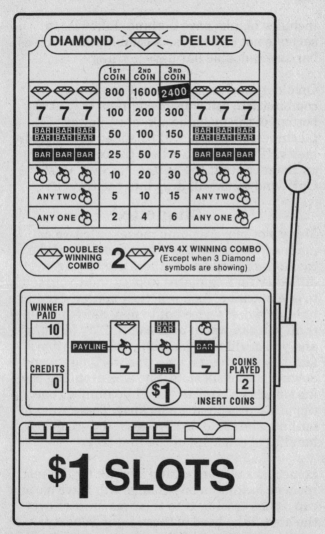

This slot machine takes up to three dollar coins, but one-armed bandits can range from nickel and quarter slots to machines that accept five dollars or more.

includes blanks pays nothing. Likewise, a seven is not any bar, so a combination such as bar-seven-double bar pays nothing.

On older machines, if you hit a winning combination, coins dropped into a tray at the bottom of the machine. On most newer machines, winnings will be added to the credit meter. If you wish to collect the coins showing on the meter, hit the button marked "Cash Out," and coins will drop into the tray.

Etiquette

Many slot players pump money into two or more adjacent machines at a time, but if the casino is crowded and others are having difficulty finding places to play, limit yourself to one machine. As a practical matter, even in a light crowd, it's wise not to play more machines than you can watch over easily. Play too many and you could find yourself in the situation faced by the woman who was working up and down a row of six slots. She was dropping coins into machine number six while number one, on the aisle, was paying a jackpot. There was nothing she could do as a passerby scooped a handful of coins out of the first tray.

Sometimes players taking a break for the rest room or looking to buy change will leave a coin cup on the stool next to their machine or over the arm. Take heed of these signs. A nasty confrontation could follow if you play a machine that has already been thus staked out.

Payouts

Payout percentages have risen since the casinos figured out it's more profitable to hold 5 percent of a dollar than 8 percent of a quarter or 10 percent of a nickel. In most of the country, slot players can figure on about a 93 percent payout percentage, though payouts in Nevada run higher. Downtown Las Vegas usually offers the highest average payouts of all—better than 95 percent. Keep in mind that these are long-term averages that will hold up over a sample of 100,000 to 300,000 pulls. In the short term, anything can happen. It's not unusual to go 20 or 50 or more pulls without a single payout. Nor is it unusual for a machine to pay back 150 percent or more for several dozen pulls. But in the long run, the programmed percentages will hold up.

The change in slots has come in the computer age, with the development of the micro-processor. Earlier slot machines were mechanical, and if you knew the number of stops—symbols or blank spaces that could stop on the payout line—on each reel, you could calculate the odds on hitting the top jackpot. If a machine had three reels, each with ten stops, and one symbol on each reel was for the jackpot, then three jackpot symbols would line up, on the average, once every $10 \times 10 \times 10$ pulls, or 1,000 pulls.

On those machines, the big payoffs were $50 or $100—nothing like the big numbers slot

SLOT HISTORY AND TRIVIA

The first recognizably modern slot machine was the Liberty Bell, invented by Charles Fey in San Francisco in 1887. The cast-iron machine had three reels with symbols based on card suits, horseshoes, and bells.

The bars that are common symbols on today's machines are based on an early-20th-century gum manufacturer's logo. To take advantage of loopholes in state laws, slots were disguised as vending machines—with each coin in, the buyer would get a stick of gum. Playing-card symbols, with their connotations of gambling, were abandoned for fruit symbols—cherries, lemons, oranges. Other early slot machines paid off in golf balls, drinks, cigarettes, or cigars.

Lemons soured many an otherwise winning combination. Today when we refer to an unsatisfactory product as "a real lemon," we're using a term derived from early slot machines.

The largest slot jackpot ever hit was $9,346,876.45 in July 1992, on a $1 machine at a casino in Reno. The largest on a quarter machine was $2,472,819 in Las Vegas in June 1993, and the largest nickel jackpot was $957,034 at a Jackpot, Nevada, casino in June 1994.

The largest slot machine in the world is an 18-foot-long, 9-foot-high machine in a Las Vegas casino. It seats six players. After all who are seated have made their wagers, a casino employee—sometimes a woman dressed in royal regalia—pulls the handle.

players expect today. On systems that electronically link machines in several casinos, progressive jackpots reach millions of dollars.

The microprocessors driving today's machines are programmed with random-number generators that govern winning combinations. It no longer matters how many stops are on each reel. If we fitted that old three-reel, ten-stop machine with a microprocessor, we could put ten jackpot symbols on the first reel, ten on the second, and nine on the third, and still program the random-number generator so that three jackpot symbols lined up only once every 1,000 times, or 10,000 times.

Each possible combination is assigned a number, or numbers. When the random-number generator receives a signal—anything from a coin being dropped in to the handle being pulled—it sets a number, and the reels stop on the corresponding combination.

Between signals, the random-number generator operates continuously, running through dozens of numbers per second. This has two practical effects for slot players. First, if you leave a machine, then see someone else hit a jackpot shortly thereafter, don't fret. To hit the same jackpot, you would have needed the same split-second timing as the winner. The odds are overwhelming that if you had stayed at the machine, you would not have hit the same combination.

Second, because the combinations are random, or as close to random as is possible to set the program, the odds of hitting any particular combination are the same on every pull. If a machine is programmed to pay out its top jackpot, on the average, once every 10,000 pulls, your chances of hitting it are one in 10,000 on any given pull. If you've been standing there for days and have played 10,000 times, the odds on the next pull will still be one in 10,000. Those odds are long-term averages. In the short term, the machine could go 100,000 pulls without letting loose of the big one, or it could pay it out twice in a row.

Strategy

Slots are the easiest games in the casino to play—spin the reels and take your chances. Players have no control over what combinations will show up or when a jackpot will hit. There is no way to tell when a machine will be hot or cold.

Still, there are some pitfalls. It's important to read the glass and learn what type of machine it is. The three major types are the multiplier, the buy-a-pay, and the progressive.

The multiplier. On a multiplier, payoffs are proportionate for each coin played—except, usually, for the top jackpot. If the machine accepts up to three coins at a time, and if you play one coin, three bars pay back ten. Three bars will pay back 20 for two coins and 30 for three coins. However, three sevens might pay 500 for one coin and 1,000 for two, but jump to 10,000 when all three coins are played. Read the glass to find out if that's the case before playing less than the maximum coins on this type of machine.

The buy-a-pay. Never play less than the maximum on a buy-a-pay, on which each coin "buys" a set of symbols or a payout line. The first coin in might allow the player to win only on cherry combination, while the second coin activates the bar payouts, and the third coin activates the sevens. Woe is the player who hits three jackpot symbols on a buy-a-pay with only one coin played—the player gets nothing back. A variation is the machine with multiple payout lines, each activated by a separate coin. All symbols are active with each coin, but if a winning combination lines up on the third-coin payout line with only one or two coins played, the payoff is zero.

The progressive. You also have no reason to play less than maximum coins on a progressive machine. A player who eventually lines up the jackpot symbols gets a percentage of each coin played. The first progressive machines were self-contained—the jackpot was determined by how much that particular machine had been played since the last big hit. Today most progressives are linked electronically to other machines, with all coins played in the linked machines adding to a common jackpot.

SLOTS OF THE FUTURE

The microprocessors and random-number generators that drive today's machines have rendered reels obsolete.

A machine with a video screen displaying likenesses of reels could be programmed to give the same results and, with fewer moving parts, would be less expensive to build and maintain. But when video slots have been tried, they've met consumer resistance. It seems slot players like to see those reels spinning. And a machine nobody plays is not cost-effective, no matter how inexpensive it is to maintain. In most places video slots have been tried, they've quickly been replaced by slots with reels.

Manufacturers are ready to try again, though, hoping that a new generation of players weaned on home video games and computers will be willing to gamble on reel simulations projected on a screen. And this time the casinos have an added incentive to give them a try. Using touch-screen technology, new machines allow a player to choose among several games on the same unit.

The idea has potential appeal for casino operators facing a space crunch. Instead of trying to work out how much of the available slot space to give to video poker and how much to reel slots, the operator can put both on the same machine. This could be particularly appealing to riverboat casinos, which have limited space.

But the question remains: Will the public accept video slots?

These jackpots can be enormous—the record is $9,346,876.45, won by a nurse on a $1 progressive at a Reno casino. The tradeoff is that frequency and size of other payouts are usually smaller. And you can't win the big jackpot without playing maximum coins.

If you must play fewer than maximum coins, look for a multiplier in which the final-coin jump in the top jackpot is fairly small. Better yet, choose a machine that allows you to stay within your budget while playing maximum coins. If your budget won't allow you to play maximum coins on a $1 machine, move to a quarter machine. If you're not comfortable playing three quarters at a time, move to a two-quarter machine. If you can't play two quarters at a time, play a nickel machine.

Money Management

Managing your money wisely is the most important part of playing any casino game, and also the most difficult part of playing the slots. Even on quarter machines, the amount of money involved runs up quickly. A dedicated slot player on a machine that plays off credits can easily get in 600 pulls an hour. At two quarters at a time, that means wagering $300 per hour—the same amount a $5 blackjack player risks at an average table speed of 60 hands per hour.

Most of that money is recycled from smaller payouts—at a casino returning 93 percent on

quarter slots, the expected average loss for
$300 in play is $21. Still, you will come out
ahead more often if you pocket some of those
smaller payouts and don't continually put
everything you get back into the machine.

One method for managing money is to divide
your slot bankroll for the day into smaller-
session bankrolls. If, for example, you've taken
$100 on a two-and-a-half-hour riverboat cruise,
allot $20 for each half-hour. Select a quarter
machine—dollar machines could devastate a
$100 bankroll in minutes—and play the $20
through once. If you've received more than $20
in payouts, pocket the excess and play with the
original $20. At the end of one half-hour,
pocket whatever is left and start a new session
with the next $20.

If at any point the original $20 for that session
is depleted, that session is over. Finish that
half-hour with a walk, or a snack, or a drink
until it is time for a new session. Do not dip
back into money you've already pocketed.

That may seem rigid, but players who do not
use a money management technique all too
frequently keep pumping money into the
machine until they've lost their entire
bankroll. The percentages guarantee that the
casino will be the winner in the long run, but
lock up a portion of the money as you go along,
and you'll walk out of the casino with cash on
hand more frequently.

SLOT MYTHS

Because most players do not understand how slot machines work, whole sets of beliefs have grown over when to play a machine and when to avoid it. Little truth is in any of them. Here's a look at some of the more pervasive slot myths:

Change machines after a big jackpot—the machine won't be due to hit again for some time: From a money-management standpoint, it makes sense to lock up the profits from a big hit and move on. But the machine is not "due" to turn cold. In fact, the odds against the same jackpot hitting on the next pull are the same as they were the first time.

Play a machine that has gone a long time without paying off—it is due to hit: Slot machines are never "due." Playing through a long losing streak all too frequently results in a longer losing streak.

Casinos place "hot" machines on the aisles: This belief is so widespread that end machines get a good deal of play regardless of how they pay. It is true that not all machines in the same casino are programmed with the same payback percentage. And it's true that casinos want other customers to see winners. But slot placement is more complex than just placing the hot ones at the ends of aisles.

The payback percentage is lowered when the crowds are bigger and demand is greater: It's not that easy to change a machine's programming. Changing the programmed payback percentage requires opening the machine and replacing a computer chip. That's not something to do cavalierly.

VIDEO POKER

In the early 1970s, when video poker was introduced and was still struggling for acceptance, the machines were usually referred to as "poker slots." And video poker has a lot in common with slot machines. They are easy to use, requiring no interaction with a dealer or with other players. Card combinations, like slot reels, are governed by a random-number generator.

But video poker adds something slot machines don't have—an element of skill. Players have decisions to make that affect the outcome. And because cards are required to be dealt from a randomly shuffled 52-card deck—or 53 cards, in the case of Joker's Wild machines—the possible combinations are known, the frequency of the combinations can be calculated, and an optimal playing strategy can be devised. In fact, when Missouri riverboats opened under a law that forbade games of chance, casinos were allowed to offer video poker, as a game of skill, even though slots, as games of chance, had to wait until voters changed the law.

The best video poker machines, played skillfully, offer odds that rival any table game. The basic game, Jacks or Better, in its full-pay version returns 99.6 percent with optimal play

over the long haul. Other machines, especially
some versions of Deuces Wild, offer a positive
expectation to the player—that is, over the
long haul, they'll return more than 100 percent
with optimal play.

Why do casinos offer games that can be
beaten? Because only a very small percentage
of players know the basics of proper play.
Enough mistakes are made that the casinos
actually pay out 2 to 4 percent less than the
expectation for skilled players. In competitive
markets, casinos walk a tightrope between two
choices—offering a pay table so good that the
best players can expect to make a profit in the
long term, or offering lower pay tables and risk
driving away the weaker players who are the
casino's bread-and-butter customers. In less-
competitive markets, where the demand for
space to play is great, casinos will offer lower-
paying machines because they will be played
despite the low payoffs.

Enough Americans have an easy familiarity
with the rank of poker hands that video poker
has become one of the most popular casino
games. As gambling markets mature and
players become more experienced, the demand
for video poker has tended to become stronger.
In Nevada, casinos with a clientele of locals
devote more than 50 percent of slot space to
video poker, and there are video poker bars
that offer few other gambling options. The
major resorts that cater to tourists turn a

lower percentage of space to video poker, about 10 percent to 15 percent. That's about the percentage you'll find in other United States gaming destinations. In Missouri, as soon as voters allowed games of chance, about 80 percent of slot space was turned over to reel slots.

The Basic Machine: Jacks or Better

Almost all video poker machines in use today are variations on five-card draw poker. Attempts have been made to introduce machines based on seven-card stud, and a few machines based on five-card stud are in use. But five-card draw is the basic game, and Jacks or Better is the most common variation.

There is no dealer's hand or no other player's hand to beat; payoffs are strictly according to a pay table posted on the machine. The lowest winning hand is a pair of jacks or better (a pair of queens, kings, or aces).

Each machine features a video screen on which the images of cards are dealt. Winnings are usually compiled as credits, which the player may cash out at any time, and the credits are also displayed on a meter on the video screen. On some machines the pay table will also be on the screen; on others, the pay table is painted on the machine's glass.

Below the screen is a console with a slot into which the player drops coins or tokens. Some

	1ST COIN	2ND COIN	3RD COIN	4TH COIN	5TH COIN
ROYAL FLUSH	250	500	750	1000	4000
STRAIGHT FLUSH	50	100	150	200	250
FOUR OF A KIND	25	50	75	100	125
FULL HOUSE	8	16	24	32	40
FLUSH	5	10	15	20	25
STRAIGHT	4	8	12	16	20
THREE OF A KIND	3	6	9	12	15
TWO PAIR	2	4	6	8	10
PAIR OF JACKS or better	1	2	3	4	5

VIDEO POKER

PLAY 1 TO 5 COINS

WIN 4000 COINS ON ROYAL FLUSH WITH 5 COINS BET

25¢ PLAY 5 COINS

HELD HELD HELD

PLAY 1 TO 5 COINS

5 COINS IN 5

CREDIT 28

CASH OUT | BET ONE COIN | HOLD CANCEL | HOLD CANCEL | HOLD CANCEL | HOLD CANCEL | HOLD CANCEL | DEAL DRAW | PLAY MAX COINS

VIDEO POKER

When choosing a video poker machine, be sure to select one with the highest payout. This machine shows a common 8-5 payout.

newer machines also have currency acceptors; the player slides a bill into the acceptor, the machine displays the number of credits the player may use to bet. Usually, on the left are buttons marked "Cash Out" and "Bet One Credit"; in the center are five buttons, one corresponding to each card dealt, marked "Hold/Cancel"; to the right is one button marked "Deal/Draw" and one marked "Bet Max."

Play begins when the player drops a coin or coins into the slot or bets credits. Most machines accept up to five coins or credits at a time. If using coins, the player may start the hand after dropping one, two, three, or four coins into the slot by hitting the Deal/Draw button. On the fifth coin, the machine will deal the hand automatically, without a push of the button. If playing credits, the player may hit the Bet One Credit button once for each credit the player wishes to bet, then hit Deal/Draw. If the player hits Bet Max, the machine will deduct five credits and deal the hand.

Once you've made your bet, five cards are dealt faceup on the screen. You have the option of holding or discarding any or all of the cards. To hold, push the Hold/Cancel button corresponding to the card you've chosen. You may hit the same button again to cancel the hold decision.

After you make all your hold decisions, you push the Deal/Draw button. All cards not held will then be discarded, and new cards will be turned up to take their places. These five cards are the final hand. The machine compares that hand to the pay table, and if the hand is a winner, the corresponding number of credits are added to the meter.

Rank of Poker Hands

All payoffs are based on five-card poker hands, which rank as follows:

Royal flush: Ace-king-queen-jack-10 all of the same suit (hearts, clubs, spades, or diamonds).

Straight flush: Five consecutive cards of the same suit; for example, 2-3-4-5-6, all of clubs.

Four of a kind: Four cards of the same rank; for example, ace of hearts, ace of spades, ace of clubs, ace of diamonds.

Full house: Three cards of one rank, two cards of another rank; for example, 3 of diamonds, 3 of hearts, 3 of spades, 6 of hearts, 6 of spades.

Flush: Five cards of the same suit; for example, ace, 10, 7, 4, 3, all of diamonds.

Straight: Five consecutive cards of mixed suits; for example, 2 of diamonds, 3 of hearts, 4 of diamonds, 5 of clubs, 6 of spades.

Three of a kind: Three cards of the same rank; for example, 6 of hearts, 6 of clubs, 6 of diamonds.

Two pair: Two cards of one rank, two cards of another rank; for example, ace of spades, ace of hearts, 7 of clubs, 7 of diamonds.

Pair of jacks or better: Two jacks, queens, kings, or aces.

These are all examples of winning hands for video poker. They include: (top row) royal flush, straight flush; (middle row) four of a kind, full house, flush; (bottom row) straight, three of a kind, two pair, and pair of jacks or better.

Etiquette

If the machine is not equipped with a currency acceptor, change currency for coins or tokens either with a change person, whose job is to move through the casino with a cart full of change, or at a change booth. In some casinos, money can also be changed at the cashier's cage. If you run out of change and want to keep playing the same machine, at most casinos you can summon a change person by pushing a button marked "CHANGE." That will turn on a light on top of the machine.

Be sure the machine you have chosen is not already in use. Sometimes players taking a rest room break or looking for change will place a coin cup on the chair by a machine or on the screen itself to signal the machine is occupied.

Confine yourself to playing one machine. The decisions in video poker require more concentration than pushing the "SPIN REELS" button on the slot machines.

The Pay Table

The version of Jacks or Better regarded as full-pay, returning 99.6 percent with optimal play, is commonly referred to as a 9-6 machine, from the 9-for-1 payoff for a full house and 6-for-1 payoff on a flush. The full table for a 9-6 machine, with returns for one coin played, is as follows: Pair of jacks or better, 1; two pair, 2; three of a kind, 3; straight, 4; flush, 6; full house, 9; four of a kind, 25; straight flush, 50; and royal flush, 250.

With one exception, payoffs are proportional to the number of coins played; that is, three of a kind returns three coins with one coin played, six for two, nine for three, 12 for four, or 15 for five. The exception comes on a royal flush, which pays 250 coins for one, 500 for two, 750 for three, 1,000 for four, but on the fifth coin jumps to a return of 4,000 coins.

Casinos usually change the machines' payout percentages by lowering the payouts on the flush and full house. In the Midwest and

VIDEO POKER HISTORY AND TRIVIA

In the early 1980s, Si Redd and his new International Gaming Technology entered into a licensing agreement with Bally's Manufacturing that gave IGT exclusive rights to manufacture video poker machines. Few people recognized the potential at the time, but that gave IGT the boost it needed to become Bally's main competitor in producing electronic gaming devices.

Today IGT and Bally's both produce video poker machines, and their machines take up most of the floor space devoted to electronic gaming devices across the country.

Until recently, some video poker machines called for the player to push a button to discard a card rather than to hold it. That caused some confusion for players moving from one type of machine to the other. Today, "HOLD" buttons are standard, though a few older machines of the "DISCARD" type remain in use.

South, 8-5 machines, paying 8-for-1 on the full house and 5-for-1 on the flush, and 7-5 machines are the most common. With optimal play, an 8-5 machine yields 97.9 percent; the 7-5 machine pays 96.2 percent.

Full-pay 9-6 machines are most common in Nevada, but their numbers are growing in Atlantic City, and 9-6 machines have been introduced at some locations in Missouri and Illinois. Even in Nevada, some casinos offer the 8-5 pay table, sometimes even alternating 9-6 and 8-5 pay tables at the same bank of machines. Be sure to read the pay table before sitting down to play. If you are in an area with several casinos within walking distance, do not settle for a pay table that is below the standard for the area.

The best Jacks or Better machines ever offered were 10-6 and 9-7 machines at a casino in Las Vegas. Both versions carried payout percentages of more than 100 percent for optimal play, a fact the casino proudly trumpeted with signs on every machine. Of course, the casino didn't lose money on these machines—most video poker players aren't skilled enough to play at optimal level.

One caution: Even a skilled player on 100-percent-plus machines will have more losing sessions than winners. Those percentages assume that over the long haul the player will hit a normal share of royal flushes with full coins played. Royal flushes are expected about once every 40,000 hands—about once every 80 hours of play. There are no guarantees, however. Without a normal number of royal flushes, or if fewer than the maximum number of coins are played, the payout percentages will be lower.

A Quick Strategy

Most video poker players can improve their chances by following the few simple rules for holding or discarding the first five cards that they have been dealt:

Always hold a royal flush, straight flush, four of a kind, full house, three of a kind, or two pair. However, with three of a kind, discard the remaining two cards for a chance at four of a kind while leaving full house opportunities open, and with two pair, discard the fifth card for a chance at a full house.

Break up a flush or a straight only when you have four cards to a royal flush. That is, if you have ace-king-queen-jack-9, all of clubs, discard the 9 to take a chance at the big payoff for the 10 of clubs. That still leaves open the possibility of a flush with any other club, a straight with any other 10, and a pair of jacks or better with any ace, king, queen, or jack.

Break up a pair of jacks or better if you have four cards to a royal flush or four cards to a lower straight flush.

Keep a low pair instead of a single high card (jack, queen, king, or ace).

Do not draw to a four-card inside straight—one in which the missing card is in the middle rather than on either end—unless it includes at least three high cards. A four-card open straight is one that has space open at either end to complete the hand; for example, a hand of 4-5-6-7 can use either a 3 at one end or an 8 at the other to complete the straight. An inside straight has space in the middle that must be filled to complete the hand; 4-6-7-8 needs a 5 to become a straight. Open straights give the player a better chance, with twice as many cards available to fill the straight.

Optimal Strategy

Once you're used to the quick strategy, you may want to move on to a version that is more complex, but more accurate. Following is a strategy that is optimal for the most common machines in the United States, 8-5 and 7-5 Jacks or Better. It also varies only a few tenths of a percent from optimal on 9-6 Jacks or Better and for Bonus Poker machines.

Just as in the quick version, a few hands are never broken up. Obviously, if you're fortunate enough to be dealt a royal flush, you hold all five cards and wait for your payoff. (On payoffs this large, the machine will flash "Jackpot!" or "Winner!" In these cases the winnings will be paid by an attendant rather than by the machine. Do not put more coins in the machine or attempt to play another hand before you are paid for the royal flush.)

Also hold all five cards on a straight flush or a full house. Hold all four matching cards on four of a kind. Hold three of a kind while discarding the other two cards for a chance at either four of a kind or a full house. Hold both pairs in a two-pair hand, but discard the fifth card for a chance at a full house.

In the right circumstances, however, the player sometimes will break up a flush, a straight, or a pair of jacks or better. If you do not have one of the "always keep" hands, use the following list. Possible predraw hands are listed in order. Find the highest listing that fits your predraw hand, and discard any cards that do not fit the hand. For example, if your hand includes jack of spades, jack of diamonds, 10 of diamonds, 9 of diamonds, and 8 of diamonds, you have four cards to an open straight flush in diamonds, and you also have a pair of jacks or better. The four-card open straight flush is higher on the list than the pair of jacks or better, so you would discard the jack of spades and draw to the four-card straight flush. You are giving up the certain 1-for-1 payoff for a pair of jacks, but you have a chance at a straight flush with either a queen or 7 of diamonds, could draw a flush with any other diamond, or still could finish with a pair of jacks by drawing the jack of either clubs or hearts.

This strategy distinguishes between inside straights or straight flushes and open straights or straight flushes.

Remember, keep a royal flush, straight flush, four of a kind, full house, three of a kind, or two pair. Here is how other predraw hands rank:

1. **Four-card royal flush.** Note that you would break up a flush, a straight, or a high pair when you're missing only one card in a royal flush. But if you have a straight flush that runs from 9 through king of the same suit, take the straight flush payoff rather than chasing the royal.

2. **Flush.**

3. **Straight.**

4. **Four-card open straight flush.** The big difference in the payoff between a royal flush and a lower straight flush means that the only winning hand you break up to chase a straight flush is a pair of jacks or better, whereas you'd also break up a flush or a straight to chase the royal. There is no option to break up two pair.

5. **Four-card inside straight flush.**

6. **Pair of jacks or better.** Discard the remaining three cards. Sometimes players who are used to playing table poker want to

keep a high-card "kicker" to the pair—for example, holding an ace along with two queens. Don't hold a kicker in video poker; give yourself the maximum chance to draw a third high card, or even a full house or four of a kind.

7. **Three-card royal flush.**

8. **Four-card flush.**

9. **Four-card open straight, two or three high cards.** An example would be 9 of clubs, 9 of spades, 10 of clubs, jack of hearts, queen of diamonds. Throw away one of the 9s, and the remaining cards give you a chance at a straight with either an 8 or a king, and you also have a chance at either a pair of jacks or a pair of queens.

10. **Low pair (two 10s or lower).** Most new players keep a single jack or better rather than a low pair, and it's true that keeping that one high card will result in more frequent winning hands. But most of those will be 1-for-1 payoffs for a pair of jacks or better. Keeping the low pair will result in more two-pair, three-of-a-kind, full-house, even four-of-a-kind hands.

11. **Four-card open straight, one high card.**

12. **Three-card inside straight flush with two high cards.**

13. **Three-card open straight flush with one high card.**

14. **Four-card open straight, no high cards.**

15. **Two-card royal flush, no Ace or 10.** You won't hit the royal most of the time, but more possible straights can be formed with lower cards than with aces. And unlike other parts of a royal flush, the 10 leaves no potential high-pair payoff. So the two-card royal is a better play with cards in the middle than with aces or 10s.

16. **Three-card double inside straight flush, two high cards.** A double inside straight flush has both cards missing on the inside; for example, 8-jack-queen of clubs, where the 9 and 10 are needed.

17. **Four high cards; ace, king, queen, and jack of mixed suits.** The draw could match any of them for a pair of jacks or better or bring a 10 for a straight.

18. **Three-card open straight flush, no high cards.**

19. **Two-card royal flush, including ace but no 10.**

20. **Four-card inside straight with three high cards.** For example, king-queen-jack-

VIDEO POKER VARIATIONS

Several variations of video poker have become popular, and new machines are being developed all the time. Be careful of gimmick machines; many offer excellent payout percentages, but the strategy is more complex than in Jacks or Better. Learn the basic game first before branching out.

Deuces Wild: Any 2 may be used to substitute as any other card. For example ace-ace-6-2-2 pays as four aces. As in Jacks or Better, the top jackpot is for a royal flush with no deuces. There also is a minijackpot of 200-for-1 for four deuces.

The hands to look for on the pay table are royal flush with deuces, five of a kind, straight flush, and four of a kind. On a full-pay machine, which returns 100.6 percent with optimal play, the payoffs for one coin will be 25-15-9-5; the more they deviate downward from those numbers, the lower-paying the machine.

Some strategy tips: There is no payoff for a pair of Jacks or Better, so do not save a single high card. If you have two pair, save only one of the pairs. Two pair returns nothing, and a three-card draw gives you a better chance at three of a kind. In a hand with two deuces, do not save a third card as a three of a kind. Any card will give you at least three of a kind with the two wild cards; go for a bigger hand. And in Deuces Wild, draw to inside straights that you would discard in Jacks or Better. Being able to fill the straight with the four deuces as well as the natural cards tips the percentages in favor of going for it.

However, if the fifth card matches one of the cards in the four-card inside straight, save the pair instead.

Bonus Poker: Most of the pay table is the same as on an 8-5 Jacks or Better machine. However, four 2s, 3s, or 4s pay 40-for-1, instead of paying 25-for-1, and four aces pay 80-for-1. The bonuses make this machine, in its 6-5 setting, approximately equivalent to an 8-5 Jacks or Better machine, with better than 97 percent payback with optimal play. At 8-5, Bonus Poker is close to a 100 percent machine.

Double Bonus Poker: All four-of-a-kind hands feature a higher payoff than in Jacks or Better—160-for-1 for Aces, 80-for-1 for 2s, 3s, or 4s, 50-for-1 for all other four-of-a-kind hands. In the full-pay version, the full house pays 10-for-1 and the flush pays 7-for-1, but it's more common to find a 9-6 pay table.

The most important strategy variation in Double Bonus Poker comes when the original five-card hand includes two pair, one of which is a pair of jacks or better. In this case, discard the low pair, because two pair pays no more than the pair of jacks or better.

Joker's Wild: A 53rd card—a joker that may substitute for any card—is added to the deck. Watch out for machines that start the pay table at two pair, with no return on a pair of kings or better. Many casinos also lower the payoff on four of a kind, full house, and flush. The wide variation in pay tables makes Joker's Wild anywhere from a 100.6 percent machine to a 94 percent machine. Strategy is much more complex than in Jacks or Better, but for starters, remember that a pair of jacks or queens is just another low pair here.

9 of mixed suits; this is the lowest ranking inside straight we draw to. With any others that do not qualify elsewhere on the list, discard all five cards. With jack-10-8-7-3, you'd keep the jack (no. 26 on the list), but with 10-9-7-6-3, you'd draw five new cards.

21. Three high cards.

22. Three-card double inside straight flush, one high card.

23. Three-card inside straight flush, no high cards.

24. Two high cards.

25. Two-card royal, includes 10 but no ace.
Note that we don't draw to two-card royals consisting of an ace and a 10. In that case, you would just keep the ace and discard the rest.

26. One high card.

27. Three-card double-inside straight flush, no high cards.

In any hand that does not fit one of the above categories, draw five new cards.

That's a pretty lengthy list for a beginner, but it can be shortened considerably by taking all those three card straight flushes—open, inside, double inside, with high cards, without high cards—and lumping them together just below four high cards. That'll cost you a few tenths of a percent, but when you're comfortable with the rest of the strategy, you can start breaking down the categories for more expert play.

Money Management

Two important points to remember: Don't overbet your bankroll, and if a machine is available at which you feel comfortable playing the maximum number of coins, do so. If you are sitting down to play with $20, you don't belong at a $1 machine that will take up to $5 at a time. It is better to play five quarters at a time than one dollar at a time. Though video poker machines pay back a high percentage of the money put into them, the payouts are volatile. It is not unusual to go five or ten or more consecutive hands with no payout. Don't play at a level at which you do not have the funds to ride out a streak.

BLACKJACK

Millions of players have heard the message that of all the casino table games, blackjack is the one that it is possible to beat. A practical system for counting cards in blackjack to gain an edge over the casino was made available to the public in the early 1960s. As it happened, few players ever really learned to beat the dealer. Furthermore, playing conditions have changed since then. Some tables use more than one deck at a time or cut a percentage of the cards out of play so that a card counter never sees them.

Even though most players don't have the skill to win consistently, the belief that blackjack can be beaten was enough to spark a boom in the game. Blackjack is by far the most popular casino table game in the United States, with more players generating more casino revenue than craps, roulette, and baccarat combined.

A lot of people don't have either the patience, persistence, and concentration necessary for card counting or the bankroll to make it effective. But they can still narrow the house advantage to less than 1 percent in blackjack. The secret is to learn basic strategy for hitting, standing, doubling down, and splitting pairs. A little time spent learning to play well can make your money go a lot farther in the casino.

Rules

Blackjack is played with one or more standard 52-card decks, with each denomination assigned a point value. The cards 2 through 10 are worth their face value. Kings, queens, and jacks are each worth 10, and aces may be used as either 1 or 11. The object for the player is to draw cards totaling closer to 21, without going over, than the dealer's cards.

The best total of all is a two-card 21, or a blackjack. Blackjack pays 3-2—that is, a two-card 21 on a $5 bet will win $7.50 instead of the usual $5 even-money payoff on other winning hands. However, if the dealer also has a two-card 21, the hand pushes, or ties, and you just get your original bet back. But if the dealer goes on to draw 21 in three or more cards, your blackjack is still a winner with its 3-2 payoff.

The game is usually played at an arc-shaped table with places for up to seven players on the outside and for the dealer on the inside. At one corner of the table is a rectangular placard that tells the minimum and maximum bets at that table, as well as giving variations in common rules. For example, the sign might say, "BLACKJACK. $5 to $2,000. Split any pair three times. Double on any two cards." That means the minimum bet at this table is $5 and the maximum is $2,000. Pairs may be split according to the rules described below, and if more matching cards are dealt, the pairs may

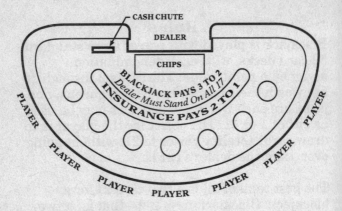

The standard table layout for blackjack.

be split up to three times for a total of four hands. The player may double the original bet (double down) and receive just one more card on any two-card total.

Most games today use four, six, or eight decks. After being shuffled, the cards are placed in a receptacle called a shoe, from which the dealer can slide out one card at a time. Single- or double-deck games, more common in Nevada than in other parts of the country, may be dealt from the dealer's hand.

Play begins when you place a bet by stacking a chip or chips in the betting square on the table directly in front of you. After all bets have been placed, each player and the dealer are given two cards. In a shoe game, all player cards are dealt faceup, and the players are not permitted to touch their cards. In a single- or double-deck game dealt from the hand, cards are dealt facedown and players may pick them up with one hand. Either way, one of the dealer's cards is turned faceup so the players can see it.

Once the cards have been dealt, players decide in turn how to play out their hands. After all players have finished, the dealer plays according to set rules: The dealer must draw more cards to any total of 16 or less and must stand on any total of 17 or more. In some casinos, the dealer will also draw to "soft" 17— a 17 including an ace or aces that could also be counted as a 7. The most common soft 17 is ace-6, but several other totals, such as ace-3-3 or ace-4-2, on up to ace-ace-ace-ace-ace-ace-ace in a multiple deck game, are soft 17s.

Hit: If you hit, you take another card or cards in hopes of getting closer to 21. If the player's total exceeds 21 after hitting, the player is said to "bust" and loses the bet. In shoe games, the player signals a hit by pointing to his cards or scratching or waving toward himself. In facedown games, the player signals a hit by scratching the table with the cards. Verbal calls to hit are not accepted—signals are used for the benefit of the security cameras above the table, so a taped record is on hand to settle any potential disputes.

Stand: If you stand, you elect to draw no more cards in hopes that the current total will beat the dealer. Signal a stand by holding a flattened palm over your cards in a faceup game or by sliding your cards under your bet in a facedown game.

Double down: You may elect to double your original bet and receive only one more card regardless of its denomination. Some casinos restrict doubling down to hands in which your first two cards total 10 or 11. Others allow you to double on any two cards. Double down by taking a chip or chips equal to the amount of your original bet and placing them next to your bet. In a facedown game, at this point you also need to turn your original two cards faceup.

Split: If your first two cards are of the same denomination, you may elect to make a second bet equal to your first and split the pair, using each card as the first card in a separate hand. For example, if you are dealt two 8s, you may slide a second bet equal to the first to your betting box. The dealer will separate the 8s, then put a second card on the first 8. You play that hand out in normal fashion until you either stand or bust; then the dealer puts a second card on the second 8, and you play that hand out.

Insurance: If the dealer's faceup card is an ace, you may take "insurance," which essentially is a bet that the dealer has a 10-value card down to complete a blackjack. Insurance, which may be taken for half the original bet, pays 2-1 if the dealer has blackjack. The net effect is that if you win the insurance bet and lose the hand, you come out even. For example, the player has 18 with a $10 bet down. The dealer has an ace up. The player takes a $5 insurance bet. If the dealer has blackjack, the player loses the $10 bet on the hand but wins $10 with the 2-1 payoff on the $5 insurance bet.

Many dealers will advise players to take insurance if the player has a blackjack. This can be done by simply calling out, "Even money"—because if the dealer does have blackjack, the player gets a payoff equal to the player's bet instead of the 3-2 normally paid on blackjack.

These are the steps involved: Player bets $10 and draws a blackjack. Dealer has an ace up. Player makes a $5 insurance bet. Dealer has blackjack. The player's blackjack ties the dealer's, so no money changes hands on the original bet. But the $5 insurance bet wins $10 on the 2-1 payoff—the same as if the original $10 bet had won an even-money payoff.

As it happens, dealers who suggest this play are giving bad advice. Insurance would be an even bet if the dealer showing an ace completed a blackjack one-third (33.3 percent) of the time. But only 30.8 percent of cards have 10-values. Taking insurance is a bad percentage play, no matter what the player

RULES VARIATIONS

Not all blackjack games are created equal. Some variations in the rules are good for the player, and some are bad. The shifts in the house edge may look small, but they make large differences in a game in which the total house edge is less than 1 percent against a basic strategy player. Here are some common variations and their effect on the house advantage:

Double downs after splitting pairs permitted: A very good rule for the player, it cuts the house advantage by .13 percent. In areas where several casinos are within reasonable distance, the player should choose games in which doubling after splits is allowed.

Resplitting of aces permitted: At most casinos, the player who splits aces receives only one more card on each ace. But if the player receives another ace, some casinos allow the resulting pair to be resplit. This option cuts the house edge by .03 percent. It is rare to find a game that goes even further by allowing the player to draw more than one card to a split ace, an option that cuts the house edge by .14 percent.

Early surrender: When the dealer's faceup card is an ace, the dealer checks to see if the down-card is a 10 to complete a blackjack before proceeding with play. If the house allows the player to surrender half the original bet instead of playing the hand before the dealer checks for blackjack, that is early surrender. A great rule for the player, and one that is rarely found, early surrender cuts the house edge by .624 percent. Surrender can easily be misused by beginners who haven't mastered basic strategy.

Late surrender: Found more often than early surrender, but still not commonplace, late surrender allows the player to give up half the bet rather than playing the hand after the dealer checks for blackjack. This decreases the house edge by .07 percent in a multiple-deck game, .02 percent in a single-deck game.

Double-downs limited to hard 11 and hard 10: Some casinos do not allow the player to double on totals of less than 10 or on soft hands. The net is a .28-percent increase in the house edge.

Dealer hits soft 17: If, instead of standing on all 17s, the dealer hits hands including an ace or aces that can be totaled as either 7 or 17, the house edge is increased by .2 percent.

Dealer takes no hole card: Cruise-ship players and visitors to Caribbean casinos will find this negative variation. The dealer gets only an up card until players have completed their hands, then plays out the hand as necessary. The negative effect comes on double-downs and split pairs. In U.S. casinos, if the dealer gets a blackjack, the house takes only the original bet. But on cruise ships and Caribbean casinos using this rule, the dealer can't check for blackjack before play is completed, and if the dealer then completes a blackjack, the house collects the added bets on double-downs and split pairs. This adds .13 percent to the house edge.

total, unless the player is a card counter who knows that an unusually large concentration of 10-value cards remains to be played.

Etiquette

When you sit down at a table, wait for the dealer to finish the hand in progress. Then you may buy chips by placing currency on the layout, pushing it toward the dealer, and saying, "Change, please."

Do not leave currency in the betting box on the table. In most newer gaming jurisdictions, casinos are not allowed to accept cash bets. However, casinos in some places allow cash bets with the call "Money plays." Don't leave the dealer wondering if that $100 bill is a request for change or a bet on the next hand.

Once you make a bet, keep your hands off the chips in the betting box until the hand is over.

If you are betting chips of different denominations, stack them with the smallest denomination on top. If you put a larger denomination on top, the dealer will rearrange them before going on with the hand. It's one way the casino guards against someone attempting to add a large-denomination chip to their bet after the outcome is known.

In multiple-deck games, give playing decisions with hand signals. In single- or double-deck games dealt facedown, pick up the cards with

one hand, scratch the table with the cards for a
hit, and slide the cards under your chips to
stand. Turn the cards faceup if you bust or if
you wish to split pairs or double down. At the
conclusion of play, let the dealer turn faceup
any cards under your chips.

If you are a novice, you might want to avoid
the last seat at the table, the one all the way to
the players' left. This is called "third base," and
the player here is the last to play before the
dealer. Although in the long run bad plays will
help other players as much as they hurt them,
in the short term other players will notice if a
mistake by the third baseman costs them
money. For example, the dealer shows a 6, the
third baseman has 12 and hits a 10 to bust.
The dealer turns up a 10 for 16, then draws a 5
for 21, beating all players at the table. The
third baseman is likely to take heat from other
players for taking the dealer's bust card
instead of standing. If you don't want the heat,
sit elsewhere.

If you wish to use the rest room and return to
the same seat, you may ask the dealer to mark
your place. A clear plastic disk will be placed in
your betting box as a sign that the seat is
occupied.

The House Edge

Because the player hands are completed first,
the players have the chance to bust before the
dealer plays. And the house wins whenever the

player busts, regardless of how the dealer's hand winds up. That is the entire source of the casino's advantage in blackjack. Because of this one edge, the casino will win more hands than the player, no matter how expert.

The casino gives back some of this advantage by paying 3-2 on blackjack, allowing players to see one of the dealer's cards, and by allowing the player to double down and split pairs. To take advantage of these options, the player must learn proper strategy.

Basic Strategy

Played well, blackjack becomes a game of skill in a casino full of games of chance. Studies of millions of computer-generated hands have

BLACKJACK TRIVIA

Blackjack's origins are European, though it's uncertain just what game is the direct ancestor. Claims have been made for the French, Spanish, and Italian games. One French game, Vingt-Un, seems the likely source for two of blackjack's nicknames, Van John and Pontoon (both corruptions of the pronunciation of the French name).

Blackjack itself is a nickname for the game of twenty-one. The nickname arose because of an early casino practice of paying a bonus on a hand consisting of the ace and jack of spades. The combination was dubbed a blackjack.

yielded a strategy for when to hit, when to
stand, when to double, when to split. This
strategy can take the house edge down to .6
percent in a six-deck game—and lower in
games with fewer decks. In a single-deck game
in which the dealer stands on all 17s and the
player is allowed to double down after splits, a
basic strategy player can even gain an edge of
.1 percent over the house. Needless to say, such
single-deck games are not commonly dealt.

Compare those percentages with players who
adopt a never-bust strategy, standing on all
hands of 12 or more so that drawing a 10 will
not cause them to lose before the dealer's hand
is played, to players who use dealer's strategy,
always hitting 16 or less and standing on 17 or
more. These players face a house edge
estimated at 5 percent—nearly 10 times the
edge faced by a basic strategy player.

Basic strategy takes advantage of the player's
opportunity to look at one of the dealer's cards.
You're not just blindly trying to come as close
to 21 as possible. By showing you one card, the
dealer allows you to make an educated
estimate of the eventual outcome and play your
cards accordingly.

One simple way to look at it is to play as if the
dealer's facedown card is a 10. Since 10-value
cards (10, jack, queen, king) comprise four of
the 13 denominations in the deck, that is the
single most likely value of any unseen card.

Therefore, if you have 16 and the dealer's up-card is a 7, you are guessing that the most likely dealer total is 17. The dealer would stand on 17 to beat your 16; therefore, you must hit the 16 to have the best chance to win.

On the other hand, if you have 16 and the dealer's up-card is a 6, your assumption would be that his total is 16, making the dealer more likely than not to bust on the next card. Therefore, you stand on 16 versus 6.

That's an oversimplification, of course, but very close to the way the percentages work out when the effect of multiple-card draws are taken into account.

The most common decision a player must make is whether to hit or stand on a hard total—a hand in which there is no ace being used as an 11. Basic strategy begins with the proper plays for each hard total faced by the player. (See the chart on the next page.)

Many players seem to hit the wall at 16 and stand regardless of the dealer's up-card. But that 16 is a loser unless the dealer busts, and the dealer will make 17 or better nearly 80 percent of the time with a 7 or higher showing. The risk of busting by hitting 16 is outweighed by the likelihood you'll lose if you stand.

Basic strategy for hard totals is straight-forward enough, but when it comes to soft

Basic Blackjack Strategy

If you have:	And dealer shows:	Do this:
8 and under	Always hit, regardless of the dealer's up-card	
9	3, 4, 5, or 6	Double down
	2 or 7 and above	Hit
10	Deuce through 9	Double down
	10 or ace	Hit
11	Deuce through 10	Double down
	Ace	Hit
12	2, 3, or 7 and above	Hit
	4 through 6	Stand
13 through 16	7 and above	Hit
	2 through 6	Stand
17 through 21	Always stand, regardless of the dealer's up-card	

totals many players become confused. They seem lost, like the player aboard a riverboat in Joliet, Illinois, who wanted to stand on ace-5—a soft 16—against a dealer's 6. The dealer asked if he was sure, and another player piped in, "You can't HURT that hand," so the player finally signaled for a hit. He drew a 5 to total 21 and was all grins.

In a facedown game, no friendly advice is available. Once, at a downtown Las Vegas casino, the dealer busted, meaning all players who hadn't busted won. One player turned up two aces and a three. "Winner five!" the dealer called out. Though it worked out that time, five (or 15) never wins without the dealer busting, and the player could have drawn at least one more card without busting. That's too big an edge to give away.

Nothing you could draw could hurt a soft 16, or a soft 15, or many other soft totals. Just as

Soft-Hand Strategies

If you have:	And dealer shows:	Do this:
Ace, ace	Split the pair of aces (see pair-splitting)	
Ace, 2 or ace, 3	5 or 6	Double down
	All other up-cards	Hit
Ace, 4 or ace, 5	4, 5, or 6	Double down
	All other up-cards	Hit
Ace, 6	3 through 6	Double down
	All other up-cards	Hit
Ace, 7	3 through 6	Double down
	2, 7, or 8	Stand
	9, 10, or ace	Hit
Ace, 8 or ace, 9	Always stand, regardless of the dealer's up-card	
Ace, 10	Blackjack—smile and take that 3-2 payoff	

with hard totals, guesswork is unnecessary. A basic strategy tells you to what to do with soft hands.

The hand of ace and 6 is the most misplayed hand in blackjack. People who understand that the dealer always stands on 17 and that the player stands on hard 17 and above seem to think 17 is a good hand, but the dealer must bust for 17 to win. If the dealer does not bust, the best 17 can do is tie. By hitting soft 17, you have a chance to improve it by drawing ace, 2, 3, or 4, or leave it the same with 10-jack-queen-king. That's eight of 13 cards that either improve the hand or leave it no worse. And even if the draw is 5, 6, 7, 8, or 9, you have another chance to draw if the dealer shows 7 or better, and you're still in position to win if the dealer busts while showing 2 through 6, and all you've given up is a chance to tie a 17.

The average winning hand in blackjack is about 19, and standing on soft 18 will lose the player money in the long run when the dealer shows 9, 10, or ace. When the dealer shows 3 through 6, the chances of the dealer busting are strong enough to make doubling down the best play here.

The final category of hands consists of those in which the first two cards match. Then the player must decide whether or not to split the pair into two hands. Basic strategy for pair splitting follows.

Pair Splitting

If you have:	And dealer shows:	Do this:
Ace, ace	Always split. When you split aces, you will get just one more card on each ace. Some casinos allow the player to split again if another ace is dealt.	
2, 2 or 3, 3	4, 5, 6, or 7	Split
	All other up-cards	Hit
4, 4	Never split. An 8 is a much stronger building block to a hand than a 4.	
5, 5	2 through 9	Never split—double down
	10 or ace	Never split—hit
6, 6	3, 4, 5, or 6	Split
	All other up-cards	Hit
7, 7	2 through 7	Split
	8 through ace	Hit
8, 8	Always split. Against a 9, 10, or ace, this is a defensive measure because 16 is such a terrible hand to play.	
9, 9	2 through 6	Split
	7	Stand, because 18 is a winner against the dealer's most likely hand, 17
	8 and 9	Split
	10 or ace	Stand
10, 10	Never split. This hand is too strong.	

Some Strategy Variations: Double Down After Splits Permitted

Many casinos allow the player to double down after splitting pairs. This is a good rule for players—in fact, any rule that allows a player an option is a good one if the player knows when to take advantage of the option. If you split 8s against a 6, for example, and a 3 is dealt to your first 8, you now are playing this hand as an 11, and it is to your advantage to double down if the house allows it.

If the casino allows doubling after splits, the following strategy variations are necessary:

If you have 2, 2; 3, 3: Split against 2 through 7 instead of 4 through 7.

If you have 4, 4: Split against 5 and 6 instead of just hitting against all.

If you have 6, 6: Split against 2 through 6 instead of 3 through 6.

Single-Deck Blackjack

You can find many single-deck games in Nevada, and they pop up occasionally in other parts of the country. You will need a few variations for single-deck blackjack. Basic strategy is much the same as in the multiple-deck game, with a few twists, given below:

If you have 11: Double down against all dealer up cards.

If you have 9: The difference comes when the dealer shows a 2. In multiple-deck you hit; in single-deck, double down.

If you have 8: Double down against 5 and 6.

If you are holding ace, 8: As good as that 19 looks, it is to the player's advantage to double down against a 6. Stand against all else.

If you are holding ace, 7: Stand against an ace, unless you are playing in a casino in which the dealer hits soft 17. In that case, hit.

If you are holding ace, 6: Double against 2 through 6.

If you are holding ace, 3 or ace, 2: Double against 4, 5, and 6.

If you are holding 2, 2: Where doubling after splits is not allowed, split against 3 through 7 in a single-deck game. Otherwise, follow the same strategy as in multiple-deck games.

If you are holding 3, 3: If doubling after splits is permitted, split against 2 through 8.

If you are holding 4, 4: If doubling after splits is permitted, split against 4 through 6.

If you are holding 6, 6: If doubling after splits is permitted, split against 2 through 7; if not, split against 2 through 6.

If you are holding 7, 7: If doubling after splits is permitted, split against 2 through 8. Also, stand against a 10 in the single-deck game.

Counting Cards

Some players seem to think counting cards means memorizing every card as it is played. If card counting were that difficult, nobody would have thought it was practical, even in the days when the basic game was single-deck with all the cards dealt out. And that kind of system certainly would have disappeared with the advent of the four-, six-, and eight-deck games that are common today. Others think counting cards is a license to print money—just memorize a counting system and go start winning. It's not that easy.

What counters do is take advantage of the constantly changing odds in blackjack. In roulette or craps, the odds are mathematically fixed to be the same on every spin of the wheel or roll of the dice. In blackjack, the odds turn in favor of the player when an unusually large number of 10-value cards remain to be played. When the deck is rich in 10s, the player gets more blackjacks and more hands of 17 or better on which to stand without risk of busting. In double-down situations, the percentage of the desirable 10-value cards for the player to hit is greater, and when the dealer's faceup card is a "stiff," or 2 through 6, it's even more likely than usual that the dealer will bust.

BETTING PROGRESSIONS

Some players who do not count cards like to increase their bets while they are winning and decrease them while they are losing. This occasionally leads to bigger wins than normal, but also makes small losses more frequent.

A $5 bettor could begin a simple progression by increasing the bet to $10 after two wins in a row. After winning two consecutive hands at the $10 level, the player would increase to $15, and so on. After any loss, the player brings the bet back down to its original level.

The progression kicks in after two consecutive wins, so that the player never loses money on any sequence that begins with a win. If, after two $5 wins, the player loses the $10 bet, he is even. A third consecutive win guarantees a profit for the sequence.

Winnings can mount fast. If a player betting a flat $5 a hand wins six hands in a row, winnings total $30. The progression bettor has won two hands at $5, two at $10, and two at $15 for $60.

However, the system has two major problems. The player always loses the largest bet in the sequence. And in any sequence that starts with two wins but shows a loss on the third hand, the progression bettor is worse off than the flat bettor. The progression bettor would be even after two $5 wins and a $10 loss; the flat bettor would show a $5 profit after two wins and a $5 loss. And a two-wins-and-a-loss sequence happens a lot more often than six consecutive wins.

Counters make no attempt to keep track of every card in the deck. They simply track the concentration of 10s and aces. When the deck is favorable to the player, they increase their bets. When the deck is favorable to the dealer, they decrease their bets.

The counting is done with a plus-and-minus system. Players who feel they are ready to tackle blackjack on an expert level might want to seek out the more complex variations suggested in the many blackjack books on the market. The most powerful systems track aces as well as 10s.

The easiest counting system available simply assigns a value of plus-one to 3s, 4s, 5s, and 6s and minus-one to 10s, jacks, queens, and kings. All other cards are treated as neutral. Every time a 3 through 6 is dealt, add one to the count. Every time a 10-value card is dealt, subtract one. The total is called the running count. For example, if ten 3s through 6s have been played and only four 10s, the running count is plus-six. This needs to be normalized to the number of decks in the game, which is done by dividing by the approximate number of decks remaining in the shoe or in the dealer's hand. In a six-deck game, if the running count is plus-six and about three decks are left in the shoe, divide plus-six by three to get a "true count" of plus-two. (Some more complex systems adjust to the number of half-decks remaining.)

The final step is to adjust the bet to the count. In this simple version, if your beginning bet is one unit of $5, when the true count reaches plus-2, bet $10; at plus-4, bet $15, and at plus-6, bet $20.

A few words of warning: Because you are increasing your bet whenever the deck is favorable, playing with a counting system requires a much larger bankroll than betting the same amount every hand—flat betting. You may be perfectly comfortable buying 10 bets' worth of chips—$10 at a $1 table or $50 at a $5 table—when flat-betting, but figure on at least 30 bets' worth when counting cards.

Card counters, just like any basic strategy player, lose more hands than they win no matter how good they are. They hope to more than make it up by winning larger bets in favorable situations. But sometimes the favorable situations just don't come—it's possible to count down six-deck shoe after six-deck shoe without ever coming across a really favorable situation. And even on positive counts, sometimes the cards just turn the wrong way. There are no guarantees, not even for those who know the count and know what to do.

Finally, if the casino thinks you're counting cards, it can take measures. Nowhere in the country is card-counting illegal, but in Nevada the courts have held that the casinos are private clubs entitled to enforce their own rules, and the casinos can bar counters from playing. In other states, players can't be barred, but the casinos can increase the percentage of cards cut out of play to render the count less accurate. They can also take measures to make the player uncomfortable—such as having a supervisor behind the table stare directly at the player while another supervisor stands at the player's shoulder from behind. If you're going to attempt to count cards, learn at home first. Deal cards to yourself or practice on a computer. Keep practicing until you're accurate every time, without moving your lips, with no brow-furrowing concentration, and without giving any other telltale signs of counting. Limit the size of your bets to a one-to-four-unit range. A larger range will spark the casino's suspicions.

CRAPS

Even blindfolded in a crowded casino, anyone can find the craps table when the dice are hot. Just follow the screams, shouts, and cheers. Jackpot winners on slot machines may be the loudest individuals in the house, but nothing is quite like the collective excitement that builds at a craps table. Whereas blackjack players are quiet studies in concentration, craps players let loose as they win or lose together.

Conversely, nothing is quite as dead as a craps table when the dice are cold. At peak hours, when you see three or four somber individuals at the big table for 24, you can be sure the loser 7s have been coming up all too frequently.

Craps is the fastest-moving of casino table games. An average speed at a busy blackjack table runs around 60 hands per hour, but the house expects about 100 decisions per hour at craps. That, along with the tendency of craps players to have several bets working at once, means that craps requires a larger bankroll than other table games. And craps offers the widest variety of bets in the casino, with dozens of wagering options on the table.

All this can be pretty intimidating to a newcomer. But casino games were not designed to chase customers away, and craps is easier than it looks at first glance. Yes, there are an enormous number of bets available, but only a few are really worth playing. And those few are among the best bets in the casino.

The Table and Personnel

Most craps tables today are double layouts. At the center of one side of the table is the boxman, who supervises the game and takes cash collected by the dealers and deposits it in a drop box. Directly opposite him is the stickman, who uses a stick to push the dice to the shooter. The stickman controls the tempo of the game. He calls out the results of each roll and keeps up a continuous patter, urging players to get their bets down.

At the center of the table between the boxman and stickman are boxes for proposition bets—one-roll bets. Also here are areas for hard-way bets—betting that a 6, for example, will be rolled as two 3s before either a 7 or any other 6 is rolled.

On the sides are two dealers who take bets, pay off winners, and collect losing bets. The players encircle these side areas. In front of the players is the "Pass" line, a bar that extends all around the table for players who are betting with the shooter. A smaller, "Don't Pass" bar is for players betting against the shooter. The areas marked "Come" and "Don't Come" are for bets similar to Pass and Don't Pass but are

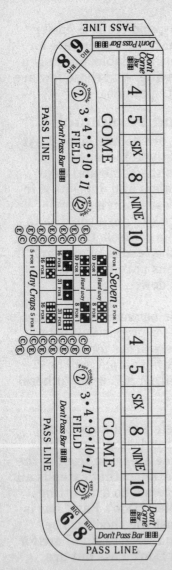

The standard craps table layout for American casinos.

placed at different times of the game. Also on the layout in front of the players is an area marked "Field" for a one-roll bet that one of seven numbers will show up. Boxes marked 4, 5, Six, 8, Nine, and 10 are for "Place" or "Buy" bets that the number chosen will be rolled before the next 7. Six and nine are spelled out because players are standing on both sides of the table—no need to wonder if that's a 6 or an upside-down 9. Down in the corner at either end of the double layout are boxes marked 6 and 8—the "Big 6" and "Big 8" bets that a 6 or 8 will roll before a 7.

Betting Sequence: the Pass/Don't Pass Wager

The betting sequence starts with the come-out roll—the first roll of the dice. The come-out roll is the time to place Pass bets, by placing a chip or chips on the Pass line directly in front of you, or Don't Pass bets, by placing a chip or chips on the Don't Pass bar. Pass bets are betting with the shooter, and Don't Pass bets are against the shooter. A player designated the shooter then flings the dice to the opposite wall of the table. If the come-out roll is 7 or 11, Pass bets win and Don't Pass bets lose. If the come-out roll is 2, 3, or 12, that's craps, and Pass bets lose. Don't Pass bets win on 2 or 3, but 12 is "barred"; Don't Pass bets neither win nor lose if the come-out roll is 12.

If the come-out is any other number, that becomes the "point." If the point number is rolled again before the next 7, Pass bets win and Don't Pass bets lose. If a 7 comes up before the point number, Don't Pass bets win and Pass bets lose. When the shooter "sevens out"—fails to make the point—the dice are passed to a new shooter. Opportunity to shoot is passed around the table clockwise.

If the shooter is coming out, a plastic disk, black side up with the word "Off" in white, will be placed in a corner of the layout, usually in a box marked "Don't come." If the disk has been flipped over to its white side, labeled "On," and placed in a numbered box, that number is the current point, and the upcoming roll is not a come-out.

"Field" bets—for a one-roll bet that one of seven numbers will show up—don't have to wait for the come-out; they may be placed before any roll by placing a chip or chips in the field area. Likewise, you may bet propositions or hard ways before any roll by putting a chip or chips on the layout and telling the dealer what bet you want.

The Best Bets

Although you may bet on any two-dice combination you can imagine, newcomers should limit themselves to the handful of bets that offer the lowest house edge:

Pass/Don't Pass: The basic bet in the game, as explained above, is also the best bet, especially when coupled with free odds. The house has only a 1.41 percent edge on a Pass bet and 1.4 percent on Don't Pass. Most players bet the Pass line, partly because they like the camaraderie of rooting for the shooter to make the point. Pass-line players are called "right bettors," as opposed to the "wrong bettors" who play Don't Pass and bet against the shooter.

The come-out is the best part of the sequence for a Pass bet—there are six ways to roll 7 with two dice and two ways to roll 11, for eight winning rolls on the come-out. And there are only four losing rolls—one way each to make 2 or 12 and two to make 3. Conversely, the come-out is the danger point for Don't Pass bets—three ways to win, since the 12 is barred, eight to lose. Once a point is established, the Don't Pass bet is the favorite to win. Pass/Don't Pass bets are paid off at even money; that is, a winning $5 bet will return your original $5 plus $5 in winnings.

Come/Don't Come: These are the same as Pass/Don't Pass, except they are placed on rolls other than the come-out. For example, if 5 is established as the point on the come-out, you now may place a Come bet by placing a chip or chips in the area marked "Come." If the next number rolled is a 7 or 11, the Come bet wins; if it is 2, 3, or 12, it loses; if it is any other number, that becomes the point for your Come bet. If a 9 is rolled, for example, the dealer moves your wager into the box marked "Nine," and if another 9 is rolled before the next 7, your Come bet wins. If the 7 comes up first, the Come bet loses. If you wish, you may then place another Come bet. Don't Come bets work exactly like Don't Pass—they lose if the next roll is 7 or 11, win on 2 or 3, push (neither win nor lose) on 12. If a point number is rolled, Don't Come bets lose if that number comes up again before the next 7 and win if the 7 comes first.

Free odds: This is paid off at true odds and is the only dead-even bet, with no house edge, in the casino. Once a point is established, a player may back a Pass or Come wager with a bet of an equal amount. This is done by placing a chip or chips directly behind a Pass-line wager. On a Come bet, the player must place the chips on the layout and tell the dealer it is odds on the Come bet. The dealer will move the odds bet into the same box as the Come number.

If the point number is rolled before the next 7, the Pass or Come wager will be paid off at even money, but the odds bet will be paid at true odds of rolling that number—6-5 on a 6 or 8, 3-2 on 5 or 9, or 2-1 on 4 or 10.

The combination of a Pass or Come bet with an odds bet lowers the house advantage to .8 percent. Modern casinos commonly offer double odds, in which the player may bet twice his original Pass or Come wager at true odds. This lowers the house edge even more, to .6 percent.

In Las Vegas, where the concentration of gambling houses sparks each to try to outdo the competition, some casinos allow odds wagers of as much as ten times the Pass or Come bet.

Don't Pass/Don't Come bettors may lay odds after a point is established, giving the house the same odds the house gives a Pass/Come bettor on an odds bet. For example, if the point is 4 or 10, a bettor with $5 on the Don't Pass line can bet another $10 to win $5 if a 7 is rolled before the point (2-to-1 odds). That might not sound like a good deal, but

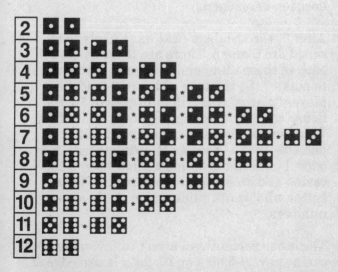

The possible dice combinations for each number can be seen here. Seven has the best chance of appearing, with six ways that it can be thrown.

remember that once a point is established,
Don't Come bettors will win more often than
they lose. Don't Come bettors who lay odds also
lower the house edge to .8 percent with single
odds, .6 percent with double odds.

Place/Buy bets: Instead of waiting for a
number to be established for Pass or Come
bets, you may place the number by putting
chips on the layout and telling the dealer what
number you want. If that number comes up
before the next 7, you win. The player may ask
the dealer to take these bets down at any time,
which cannot be done with Pass/Come bets.
Pass/Come bets remain in effect until a
decision is reached.

After 7, the numbers next most likely to be
rolled are 6 and 8. There are five ways to roll
each of these numbers, compared with six ways
to make 7. So the true odds are 6-5. If the
player "places" 6 or 8 in multiples of $6, the
house will pay winning wagers at odds of 7-6.
That leaves a house percentage of 1.52
percent—not as good as Pass/Come with free
odds, but better than most other bets in the
casino and an acceptable alternative for a
bettor who wants quick action on these two
numbers.

The other percentages aren't as favorable: The
casino pays 9-5 on 4 or 10, for a house edge of
6.67 percent, and pays 7-5 on 5 or 9 for an edge
of 4 percent.

Place Bets

Number	Payoff	True Odds	House Percentage
4	9-5	2-1	6.67%
5	7-5	3-2	4.0%
6	7-6	6-5	1.52%
8	7-6	6-5	1.52%
9	7-5	3-2	4.0%
10	9-5	2-1	6.67%

Alternatively, the player may "buy" a number by paying the house a 5 percent commission on the wager. In exchange, the casino pays Buy bets at true odds. Since the house edge is less than 5 percent on 5, 6, 8, and 9, it doesn't pay to buy these numbers. However, buying the 4 or 10 can reduce the house edge to 4.76 percent.

Unless the player tells the dealer his numbers are "working," Place and Buy bets are usually off on a come-out roll. The bets will stay in the appropriate numbered box, but if the shooter rolls a 6 on the come-out, there will be no payoff for Place bets on 6. This is so that a 7 that's a winner on the Pass line does not also wipe out all the Place bets.

Other Bets

Hard ways: There are four hard-way numbers—4, 6, 8, and 10. The number is rolled the hard way when both dice come up on the same number—that is, a hard 6 is two 3s. On a hard-way wager, the number chosen must come up hard before a 7 or before the number shows up any other combination. House edge is 11.1 percent on the 4 or 10, 9.09 percent on the 6 or 8.

Proposition bets: These are one-roll bets. A bet on any craps, for example, wins if the next roll is 2, 3, or 12; it loses if any other number is rolled. House percentages are huge: 16.67 percent on any 7, 13.9 percent on 2, 13.9 percent on 12, 11.1 percent on 3, 11.1 percent on any craps, 16.67 percent on 2 or 12, 16.67 percent on 3 or 11, 11.1 percent on 11. These are all very fast ways to lose money. Avoid them.

The Odds on Making One-Roll Propositions

Number	Ways to Roll	True Odds	House Pays	House Pct.
2	1	35-1	30-1	13.89%
3	2	17-1	15-1	11.1%
7	6	5-1	4-1	16.67%
11	2	17-1	15-1	11.1%
12	1	35-1	30-1	13.89%
Any craps 2, 3, or 12	4	8-1	7-1	11.1%

Field: Another one-roll bet, the field pays even money on 3, 4, 9, 10, or 11 and 2-1 on 2 or 12.

CRAPS TRIVIA AND SUPERSTITIONS

Opposite sides of dice—tops and bottoms—always add up to 7. That is, 1 is opposite 6, 2 opposite 5, and 3 opposite 4. Adjacent sides never add up to 7.

Dice can be rotated so that 1, 2, and 3 come into view in succession, then turned so that 4, 5, and 6 come up in rotation. It's an anticheating device, so that players and casino personnel know dice with all numbers are in the game.

Casinos do not use dice with round corners. Modern dice have square corners and are manufactured to a tolerance of 1/10,000th of an inch.

Dice made from sheep's knuckles have been found at archaeological sites, including a die with 4s on two faces found at a Roman site.

Superstitious players consider it bad luck to change dice in the middle of the roll. If, in the middle of a hot roll, the shooter throws one or both of the dice off the table, he'll often call "Same dice," just to make sure.

Don't be surprised if the table clears if a player yells out "Seven." The word is considered unthinkable, let alone unspeakable.

A penny thrown under the table is supposed to be good luck. More likely, it's just a lost penny.

It's supposed to be bad luck to throw both dice in the air while preparing to shoot. Toss one up and you'll look like an old pro; toss both and you'll have 'em heading for the exits.

With so many numbers working, this is a very popular bet, but the house edge is 5.5 percent. A few casinos pay 3-1 on the 12, lowering the edge to 2.7 percent. That's not great by craps standards, but it takes the field bet below the house percentage in most other games.

Big 6/Big 8: These work much like placing the 6 or 8—a Big 6 bet wins if a 6 is rolled before the next 7. Unlike the place bets, Big 6 and Big 8 are usually paid at even money instead of 7-6. That gives the house a 9.09 percent edge. Don't make these bets—place the 6 or 8 instead.

Etiquette

To buy chips, place currency on the layout before the shooter is given the dice, and ask the dealer for "change only." Do not try to hand cash to the dealer—the dealer is not allowed to take cash or chips directly from a customer's hand.

You may make Pass/Don't Pass bets, the odds bets backing them, and Come bets yourself by placing chips in the appropriate spaces on the layout in front of you. You also may make field bets by placing chips in the field yourself. On other bets, place chips on the layout and ask the dealer to make the bet. Once you've made your bets, pick your hands up out of the table area. Remember, craps moves fast, and you don't want to disrupt the game by deflecting the dice with your hands.

CRAPS TALK

"Comin' out. Bet those hard ways. How about the C and E? Hot roll comin', play the field. Any mo' on yo?"

A fast-talking stickman goes hand in hand with the rapid game of craps. Listening to the chatter, a novice player may have no idea what it's all about. In the example above, the stickman is letting players know that the next roll is a come-out and is urging bets on the hard ways; the one-roll proposition on craps or 11 (C and E); the one-roll bet on the field of 2, 3, 4, 9, 10, 11, and 12; and on the one-roll bet on 11 (yo, or yo-leven).

Once the roll has been made, you'll hear something like, "Winner seven!" (a 7 has been rolled, Pass line bets win) or "Seven, line away, pay the Don't" (a 7 has been rolled, Pass line bets lose and Don't Pass bets win). Many casinos prefer this call to "Loser seven," meaning the same thing, because they want to emphasize the winning Don't bets without forcing the ugly word "loser" into the minds of customers.

Every stickman has his or her own style, and some invent calls for dice combinations. But most calls are well-established throughout the United States.

The table has rails all the way around for players to store their chips. Keep yours directly in front of you, and keep your eye on them. Some players have been known to sneak a chip when another player is not looking.

When you are the shooter, you must fling the dice hard enough to hit the far wall of the table. The table supervisors will want to see the dice in the air—you may not skid them along the layout.

Cheer the shooter, root for the point to come up, be as loud as you like—provided you are betting with the shooter. Don't Pass bettors are not encouraged to join in the revelry. They are betting opposite most of the players at the table, and right bettors have been known to take it personally when a wrong bettor openly roots for them to lose. A player who lets loose with a loud "Come on, seven!" is likely to endure glares from the rest of the table.

Strategy

You'll be facing the minimum house edge at all times if you start with a Pass or Don't Pass, followed by two Come or Don't Come bets, all backed with odds bets as large as the house will allow. If you're on a winning streak, you might increase to three Come bets following the Pass bet.

Alternatively, players anxious to have the most common numbers working could start with a Pass bet, and if the point number is anything other than 6 or 8, then make place bets on those numbers. But keep in mind that the percentages aren't as good this way, and the Pass/Come method will have better results in the long run.

Craps requires a larger bankroll than most casino games. At a table with $5 minimum bets in a casino offering double odds, a player making the best percentage wagers at any given time will have $5 on the Pass line backed

CRAPS LINGO

Craps	2, 3, or 12
Yo, or Yo-leven	11
C and E	Craps or 11
Snake eyes	Two 1s
Boxcars	Two 6s. Though the public is familiar with both snake eyes and boxcars, most stickmen don't use them very often. The more common calls would be "Two, craps," or "12, craps."
Little Joe, or Little Joe from Kokomo	4, particularly rolled as a 1 and a 3
Jimmy Hicks	The number 6
Skate and donate	8
Skinny Dugan	A loser 7
Center field	9, because it's in the middle of the seven numbers on the field bet
Puppy paws	Two 5s—though the more common call is simply "Hard 10," or "10, the hard way"
Natural	Winner 7 or 11 on the come-out roll

with $10 in odds, and perhaps two Come bets with odds in the same amounts. That's $45 on the table, all of which could be wiped out by one 7 roll. A player making $5 minimum bets at blackjack or baccarat will never be in position to lose so much at once. On the other hand, if the point numbers are 4, 5, and 6, and all come up before a 7, the player could see a return of $62 plus the original $45. Craps is the table game with the most potential for fast, large wins.

A few gambling jurisdictions have $1 minimum tables with proposition bets for as little as 25 cents. But in much of the country, $5 minimum tables are as low as they go. A couple of bad sequences at these tables can wipe out a $100 bill in no time. To have enough cushion to wait out the inevitable bad streaks, figure on buying in at a $5 table for at least $100, with another $500 in reserve for the session.

ROULETTE

On the grand scale of American casino games, roulette has one of the smallest followings, with nowhere near the popularity of slot machines, video poker, blackjack, or craps. It draws more players than baccarat, mostly because the baccarat pits have traditionally been closed to low-budget players. But roulette is in danger of being passed in popularity by newer games such as Caribbean Stud Poker and Let It Ride. In Europe, on the other hand, roulette draws big crowds. It is one of the mainstays of Monte Carlo and other European resorts.

The difference is the 00 featured on the American wheel, which is not placed on the French wheel in use at European casinos. The French wheel has 36 numbers plus a single 0; the American wheel has 36 numbers plus 0 and 00. All bets at both wheels are paid at odds that would be true if only the 36 numbers existed. The house advantage in roulette comes from the 0 on the French wheel and the 0 and 00 on the American wheel.

The bottom line is that American roulette players buck a house edge of 5.26 percent on all bets but one, which carries a 7.89 percent house edge. European players face only a 2.7 percent edge, and that is lowered to 1.4 percent on even-money bets by a rule called *en prison,* which is described later in this chapter. At 1.4 percent, roulette becomes competitive with other casino games; at 5.26 percent, it's a very difficult game to beat.

A few French wheels are in use in the United States. One is a feature of a Monte Carlo-type casino area in Las Vegas; others come and go in Nevada and Atlantic City. They usually carry larger minimum bets than American wheels—but a player in these areas who plans to make larger bets and wants to play roulette should seek out a French wheel.

Even at the higher house advantage on an American wheel, most casino-goers sit in for a few spins sooner or later. It can be an entertaining, relaxing way to spend some time. The dealer—the French may call them croupiers, but in the United States they're dealers—gives players plenty of time to choose among the dozens of available betting combinations; then it takes time to spin the wheel and the ball before a winner is determined. So while craps moves at 100 or so rolls per hour and blackjack about 60 hands per hour, roulette moves at a more stately pace—roughly 45 spins per hour. Facing fewer decisions per hour, the roulette player who bets $5 per spin faces an expected loss per hour only slightly higher than that of an average blackjack player who has not learned basic strategy.

SAY IT IN FRENCH

When the dealer is a croupier and the wheel has only one 0, roulette wagers usually are referred to in French. Here are the French terms, with their English equivalents.

English	French
Red	Rouge
Black	Noir
Odd	Impair
Even	Pair
Low (1 through 18)	Manque
High (19 through 36)	Passe
Single number	En plein
Split	À cheval
Street	Transversale
Corner	Carré
First four numbers (0, 1, 2, 3)	Quatre première
Double street	Sixaine
Dozen	Douzaine
Column	Colonne
First (for dozens or columns)	Première
Middle	Moyenne
Last	Dernière

Equipment and Table Personnel

Roulette is played at an elongated table. At one end is a wheel, with a notch in the table where the dealer stands. The table is covered with a felt layout with boxes for the numbers 1 through 36 arranged in three columns and 12 rows. At the end of the portion of the layout closest to the dealer, above the numbers 1, 2, and 3, are boxes for 0 and 00. Each of the numbers 1 through 36 is surrounded by either a red or black oval or rectangle. The 0 and 00 have green backgrounds. This rectangular grid, with a box for each number, is used for wagers called "inside bets."

Outside the numbered boxes are several other boxes for "outside bets," encompassing up to 18 numbers at a time. Most of the areas for outside bets are on the long side of the table across from the dealer. However, at the end of the rectangle away from the dealer are boxes for bets on each 12-number column.

The wheel itself has 38 numbered slots, each with the same colored background as the corresponding number on the table layout. The small, hard ball used to be made of ivory; now it is usually plastic. The dealer spins the wheel in one direction, then spins the ball in the opposite direction around a track on the bowl-shaped recess that holds the wheel. When the speed of the ball decreases, it falls off the track toward the wheel itself, and bounces around until it settles in a numbered slot.

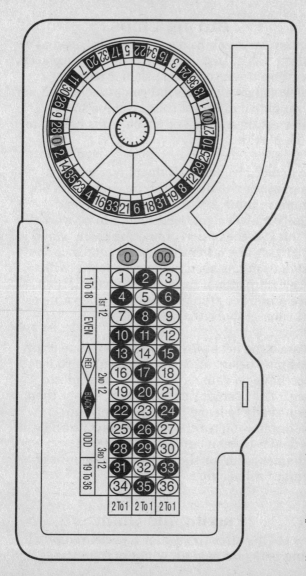

You can tell an American roulette wheel by the 00. A French wheel would be missing this number.

Buying Chips

Regular casino chips are not usually used at a roulette table. Instead, when the player places money on the layout and asks for chips, the dealer will give out special roulette chips. Each player gets a different color of chips so the dealer can keep track of which chips belong to which player.

The dealer also will ask the player what denomination to designate the chips. At a $5 minimum table, for example, the player usually may designate each chip to be worth $1, but has the option of making them worth $5, $10, or any other denomination. Once the designation has been made, the dealer will place a chip atop a rail near the wheel, then place a marker atop it to indicate the value of that color chip for that session.

Because the next player to use the same color chips may designate a different value, roulette chips have no value away from the roulette wheel. The cashier's cage will not accept them. When ready to leave the table, place all remaining roulette chips on the layout and ask the dealer to cash out. The dealer will exchange them for the equivalent amount of regular casino chips.

Playing the Game

Play begins after the dealer has cleared off all losing bets and paid all winners from the previous spin. Players are given time to put down bets by placing chips on the layout before the dealer starts the spin. After the spin has begun, players may keep betting until the ball is about to drop from the track at the top of the wheel down toward the numbered slots. Then the dealer will call, "No more bets."

The ball will bounce around, then finally settle in one slot. Next the dealer will place a marker on the layout on the corresponding number—or on top of any chips that have been bet on that number. The dealer will then clear away all losing bets and pay off all those who have bet on the winning number or on combinations including the winning number. When all that is done, the dealer will lift the marker off the number on the layout, and betting may begin again.

Etiquette

Seats at the roulette table are for players only. Even if a nonplayer sits down when only one player is at the table, the dealer will ask the nonplayer to move.

Because the house does not want to get in a dispute over what chips belong to whom, couples or friends playing together may not share chips. Even husbands and wives playing together are required to play separate colors.

Watch for your payoffs. On winning inside bets, most dealers will push the winnings to you but leave the original bet in place. After the dealer has finished payoffs and is ready for the next round of bets, it is up to you to move the original bet if you do not want to make the same wager. Some dealers will leave the winnings on the layout, and if you do not wish to bet it all on the next spin, you must remove it. It is common for the dealer to leave the winnings on outside bets next to the original bet. It is up to you to move the chips when the dealer is ready.

The Bets

Each table will carry a placard describing the minimum and maximum bets at the table. For example, it might read, "Roulette. $5 minimum inside bets, $5 minimum outside bets. $1,000 maximum outside, $100 maximum inside." Table maximums usually are lower on inside bets because of the higher payoffs offered. The odds are exactly the same as on outside bets, but most casinos are loath to risk losing $35,000 at one shot on a $1,000 bet on one number.

Though the listed minimums for inside and outside bets are likely to be the same, they don't mean the same thing. A player betting the $5 minimum on inside bets is allowed to spread five $1 chips around on different bets on the inside. However, the minimum for outside bets means the player must wager the entire $5 on each outside bet. Betting $1 on evens, $1 on red, $1 on the first 12, $1 on the first 18, and $1 on the first column doesn't satisfy the minimum.

The player may make any of the bets by placing a chip or chips on the appropriate spot. However, the size of the table may make it difficult to reach some betting areas. To place a bet you can't reach, put the chips on the table and ask the dealer to put them on the desired bet for you.

These are all examples of typical inside wagers for roulette. They include single number (4), split (5 and 6), street (1, 2, and 3), corner (2, 3, 5, and 6), five-number (0, 00, 1, 2, and 3), and double street (1, 2, 3, 4, 5, and 6) bets.

Outside Bets

Red or black: There are 18 numbers with red backgrounds and 18 with black backgrounds. A bet on red pays off if the ball stops in the slot by any of the 18 red numbers; a bet on black pays off if the ball lands on any of the black numbers. A winning red or black bet pays even money—the player keeps the original bet and gets an equal amount in winnings.

Odd or even: Another even-money bet. The player is betting that either one of the 18 odd numbers (1, 3, 5, and so forth) or one of the 18 even numbers (2, 4, 6, and so forth) will be chosen.

1 through 18, 19 through 36: Also for even money, a bet on whether the ball will stop on any of the first 18 numbers or any of the last 18 numbers.

The house gets its edge from 0 and 00—they are neither red nor black, neither odd nor even, neither part of the first 18 nor the last 18. If the ball lands on 0 or 00, all even-money bets—in fact, all outside bets—lose.

In casinos offering a French wheel with the *en prison* rule, the player does not lose an even money bet when the 0 comes up. Instead, the bet is "in prison"—the player does not lose the wager, but it remains in effect for the next spin. If the bet wins on the next spin, it is released, and the player may pull it back. The bet may not remain in prison on consecutive spins—a second consecutive 0 makes the bet a loser. This is a very favorable rule for the player, and one that is rare in the United States.

Dozens: Wagers on the first 12 numbers, second 12, or third 12 pay 2-1.

Columns: Wagers on any of the three columns on the grid pay 2-1. Because the grid is arranged in 12 rows of three consecutive numbers (1-2-3 is the first row, 4-5-6 the second, and so on), each number in a column is three higher than the one before.

Inside Bets

Single number: Bets on individual numbers, including 0 and 00, are placed by putting a chip or chips fully inside a numbered box. If a single-number bet hits, it pays 35-1. (Remember, however, that the true odds are 37-1.)

Split: This is a wager on two numbers, and it pays 17-1. Make a split bet by placing a chip so that it straddles the line between two numbers.

Street: A three-number bet, paying 11-1, is made by placing a chip on the line separating outside bets from the inside, indicating a row of three consecutive numbers.

Corner: A chip is placed at the intersection of a horizontal line with a vertical line inside the layout. This indicates a bet on the four adjacent numbers, and it pays 8-1.

Five-number: For the worst bet on the table, place a chip so that it lies on the line separating the inside from the outside, while straddling the horizontal line between 0-00 and 1-2-3. This bet pays 6-1 and carries a 7.89 percent house edge. The five-number bet does not exist on the French wheel because of the absence of 00.

Double street: Just as on the street bet, place a chip on the line separating the outside from the inside, but let it straddle the horizontal line between two rows. That gives you six numbers in two consecutive three-number rows, and the bet pays 5-1.

Strategy

Roulette is a game of pure chance, and barring exceptional circumstances, no strategy can overcome the built-in house percentage. Play your birthday, your anniversary, last week's winning lottery numbers—in the long run, it makes no difference. Either you get lucky or you don't. For most players, roulette has no element of skill.

That being said, rare exceptions do exist. Sometimes a bored longtime dealer gets in a groove and releases the ball at exactly the same angle and velocity nearly every time. A very small number of players can spot what numbers are passing as the dealer releases the ball. With that knowledge, they can predict at a better-than-chance rate approximately where the ball will fall. The player then either bets or signals a partner to bet accordingly.

The second exception comes when the wheel itself shows a bias. Perhaps the wheel is off balance, or a slight track has been worn on the wood leading down to the numbers, or the metallic walls, or frets, between numbers are of slightly different heights or tensions. This is rare, for most casinos check the wheel carefully on a regular basis. And spotting a truly biased wheel means tracking play for thousands of spins—the same number showing up three

BREAKING THE BANK

The famous "Man Who Broke the Bank at Monte Carlo" was an English engineer, Charles Jagger, who discovered a biased wheel. Jagger and his associates recorded all the numbers that came up on the wheels at the Beaux-Arts Casino Monte Carlo for several days in 1873. Jagger waded through the statistics until he found a bias on one wheel. Over several days, he continually played the biased numbers, along with others to throw casino personnel off the track. Jagger won more than $400,000.

Finally the casino discovered that the bias was caused by the frets, or walls, between numbers. The problem was corrected, and Jagger began to lose, but still left Monte Carlo, never to return, with more than $300,000.

times in half a dozen spins does not mean the wheel is biased.

Many casinos now have an electronic display at roulette wheels showing the last 12 numbers. Some players like to play any number that shows up twice or more in that span—or to bet the last several numbers that have come up—in hopes that the wheel is biased. Others like to match the bets of any other player at the table who has been winning, hoping the other player has discovered a bias. Neither system is likely to pay off, but they're as good as any other system.

Betting Systems

Perhaps because roulette moves more slowly than other casino games, players seem more inclined to use betting systems, especially on even-money bets. In the long run, none of them helps. No betting system can change the game's percentages, and some systems can be financial disasters for the player. Here are a few that have persisted for decades.

Martingale: The player doubles his bet after each loss. When a win eventually comes, it leaves the player with a profit equal to his original bet. That is, if the player bets $5 on black and loses, he then bets $10; if that loses, he bets $20, and so on. A win at the $20 level overcomes the $5 and $10 losses and leaves the player with a $5 profit. The player then goes back to the original bet level.

This sounds good in theory—keep betting until you win once, and you have a profit. In practice, you run into very large numbers very quickly, and run up against maximum bet limits. Staying with the $5 starting point, the fourth bet is $40, then $80, $160, $320. If the table maximum is $500, you're past it on the next bet—after seven losses, you cannot bet the $640 necessary to wipe out the $635 in previous losses and start a new sequence.

Streaks of seven or more losses do happen about once in every 121 sequences, and you have no way to tell when a streak is going to happen. And on that eighth bet, the house still has a 5.26 percent edge, as it does on every spin. The wheel has no memory—it does not know that seven consecutive red numbers have come up—and the streak does not change the odds on the next spin.

Besides that, having lost $635, do you really want to risk $640 more for a $5 profit?

Grand Martingale: This is an even worse, even faster way to lose money. Instead of merely doubling the bet, after a loss the player doubles the bet and adds another unit. So if the starting unit is $5, the next bet is $15 ($5 doubled, plus another $5 unit), followed by $35, then $75, $155, and so on. The Grand Martingale player runs up against a $500 limit after only six losses, by which time he will have lost $600.

HISTORY AND TRIVIA

Roulette traces its roots to the invention in England in about 1720 of the horizontal gambling wheel for a game called roly poly, which featured white and black slots, but no numbers. The first modern roulette wheels were in use in Paris by 1796.

Until the late 1800s, roulette wheels in the United States featured 31 numbers, plus 0, 00, and an American Eagle symbol that acted as a third 0.

Numbers on the wheel are arranged so that red alternates with black, odd alternates with even, and consecutive numbers of the same color add up to 37—most of the time. A perfect arrangement is impossible, because the 18 even numbers add up to 342, but the odd numbers total only 324. So two 37 totals—9 (red) plus 28 (black), and 10 (black) plus 27 (red)—include one red and one black number.

The 0, with its green background, has black numbers (2 and 28) on either side, and the 00, also on green, has red numbers (1 and 27) on either side. Using zero as a starting point on either side, the numbers alternate black-red until they reach zero.

The most frequently played single number in roulette is 17. Why? Because that's the number James Bond played in the movies.

Cancellation: Not as dangerous as the Martingales, but no solution, either. The player starts with a number or series of numbers and bets the total on either end. If he wins, he crosses off—cancels—the numbers just played. If he loses, he adds the total just played to the end of the series. When all numbers have been canceled, the result is a profit equal to the sum of the original numbers.

For example, let's say our $5 bettor starts with the series 2-3 for the $5 starting point. If he wins, he has a $5 profit and starts a new series. If he loses, the series becomes 2-3-5, and the next bet is $7—the sum of the numbers on either end. A win at $7 would cancel the 2 and the 5, leaving $3 as the next bet. A win at $3 completes the $5 profit.

All very tidy, but a perfectly ordinary sequence such as a loss, a win, two losses, a win, three losses brings the sequence to 3-3-6-9, with a $12 bet on the line and two wins needed to close out the sequence. The cancellation player doesn't run into the huge sums of money a Martingale player must bet, but can wind up making bets considerably larger than the starting point and running up losses.

BACCARAT

Derived from the European games of chemin de fer and punto banco, baccarat is a game of mystery to most of the betting public even though it's a staple of American casinos.

Baccarat comes closer than most other casino games to offering the customer an even break, with house edges of just 1.17 percent for a bet on the banker hand and 1.36 percent for a bet on the player hand. Blackjack players who use basic strategy do better; as do craps players who stick to Pass/Come bets with odds—and some casinos offer video poker machines with better percentages for a skilled player. But baccarat is a game with no playing strategies to master. The average baccarat player is at less of a disadvantage than average blackjack or video poker players and is also better off than a craps player who can't stay away from the poor-percentage bets.

Nevertheless, the game is familiar to only a relative handful of customers. For decades it was kept under wraps, played in lavish high-roller pits for the amusement of millionaires. The lowest minimum bet in the baccarat pit usually was $20, and at that the customer would feel like a piker near the likes of the late Akio Kashiwagi, who once accepted a challenge to a $12 million freeze-out at an Atlantic City casino. With $200,000-maximum bets, Kashiwagi was challenged to play until he'd either lost the $12 million or won $12 million from the casino. Six days later, with Kashiwagi having played 12 hours a day, the challenge was called off, and Kashiwagi left $10 million behind.

In casinos that cater to high rollers, baccarat has long been the game of the "whales"—the highest of the high rollers. The full-scale version is played in a separate, roped-off area at a table for 15 players, run by three dealers—none of whom actually deals the cards out of the shoe holding the eight decks. A ceremonial passing of the shoe allows players in turn to slide out the cards. This is a remnant of earlier versions of the game in which the player

HISTORY AND TRIVIA

Baccarat is the French spelling for the Italian word baccara, or zero, signifying the point values of face cards.

The game has been traced to 1490, when the Italian baccara was introduced into France, where it was a favorite of nobles during the reign of King Charles VIII.

Baccarat was first offered in Las Vegas in 1959, about a year and half after chemin de fer was introduced. Both games already were flourishing in illegal casinos in the East.

holding the shoe banked the bets of the other players.

In the 1980s, casinos began to reach out to the average customer with mini-baccarat, played on a seven-player, blackjack-sized table on the casino floor with the rest of the table games. It moves faster than baccarat, the shoe-passing ceremony has been eliminated, and the dealer deals all cards, but the rules are the same. Now anyone with $10 for a minimum bet, even $5 in some casinos, can play the game of the whales.

Banker vs. Player

Regardless of how many people are playing, only two hands are dealt. One is designated the banker hand, the other is the player hand. Any customer may bet on either hand, with the exception that the customer holding the shoe in the full-scale game must either bet banker or pass the shoe. Do not think of the bank hand as belonging to the house or the player hand belonging to the bettor. To avoid confusion, we'll refer to baccarat "bettors" or "customers" rather than "players."

Equipment and Personnel

At the full-scale, 15-player baccarat table, one dealer—the "callman"—stands up. The callman turns cards faceup after they are dealt by the bettor holding the shoe. The callman is responsible for calling out the point totals of each hand and announcing whether either

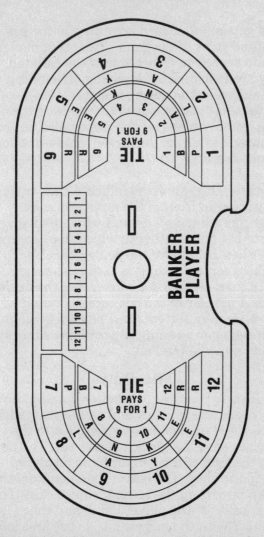

This layout is typical for baccarat. Some casinos have traditional tables that can accommodate up to 15 players.

hand gets another card according to the set hit/stand rules of the game. Two other dealers remain seated on either side of the callman. They are responsible for paying off winning bets and collecting losing wagers. Mini-baccarat has just one dealer, who deals the cards and combines all the responsibilities of the three dealers at the larger table—but does it much faster.

At either table, numbers indicate each customer position. In front of the numbers, each bettor has a lined-off area in which to place a banker bet and another in which to place a player bet. In front of the dealer are also numbers corresponding to each customer. Each time a customer wins a banker bet, the dealer places a marker in the box corresponding to that customer. Bettors must pay a 5 percent commission on winning banker bets, so these wagers must be tracked.

The Play

In full-scale baccarat, the bettor holding the shoe slides one card out and passes it facedown to the stand-up dealer, who passes it to the customer with the largest player bet. The next card, the first of the banker hand, is placed next to the shoe. The bettor then deals another player card, then the second banker card. The dealer calls for the player hand, and the customer with the largest player bet first looks at the cards, then gives them to the dealer. The dealer turns the cards faceup and announces the point total. Then the dealer calls for the banker hand, and the shoe holder looks at the cards and gives them to the dealer. If the player total requires a draw, the dealer will say, "Card for the player," and the shoe holder will pass a card to the dealer, who will pass it to the player-bettor, who looks at it and passes it back to the dealer, who turns it faceup. Finally, if the banker requires a card, the dealer will call, "Card for the bank," and repeat the process with the shoe holder.

The casino is more than willing to offer the time-consuming ceremony to its largest bettors. In mini-baccarat, however, the dealer plays out both hands, with no fuss and in half the time.

The object is to bet on the two- or three-card hand that totals closer to nine. Tens and face cards all are worth zero points; all other cards are worth their face value, with the ace worth one point. If a total is more than 10, the second digit is the value of the hand. For example, a 9 and a 6, which total 15, make up a five-point hand.

Initially, two cards are dealt for each hand. The point totals determine whether either hand gets a third card. The player hand is completed first. A total of 8 or 9 is called a "natural," and the player hand gets no more cards. In fact, unless the banker has a natural 9 or ties the natural 8, no further cards are drawn, and the

CHEMIN DE FER

The direct ancestor of baccarat as played in the United States, chemin de fer is so similar that full-scale baccarat pits are frequently marked "Baccarat/Chemin de Fer." One major difference is that the customers bet among themselves, rather than against the casino, with the house taking a commission from the customer holding the bank.

Play begins with an auction. The bettor with the highest bid becomes the first banker and puts up an amount equal to his bid as the bank, against which other bettors may bet. Wagers by all other bettors are limited to a total no higher than the bank. Any bettor may supersede all other player bets by calling, "Banco." That means the bettor is placing a bet equal to the entire bank. Each time the player hand wins, the shoe is passed, and each bettor, in turn, has the option to buy the bank and become the banker.

The other major difference from baccarat is that there are optional plays. The bettor with the largest player bet may either stand or draw on a two-card total of 5. The banker has options when holding a 3 if the player draws a 9 or when holding a 5 if the player draws a 4.

Chemin de fer was offered in Las Vegas briefly in the 1950s, but it was quickly replaced by baccarat. Today it remains popular in European casinos.

naturals are automatic winners. Player also stands on totals of 6 or 7. On any other total, zero through 5, player draws a third card, unless banker has a natural, in which case the bank hand wins with no further draw.

Banker rules are a bit more complex. Banker also stands on 7, 8, or 9 and draws on 0, 1, or 2, but on other hands the banker's play is dependent on the value of the player's third card. Banker hits 3 unless the player's third card is an 8; hits 4 unless the player's third card is 1, 8, 9, or 10; hits 5 only if the player's third card is 4, 5, 6, or 7; and hits 6 only if the player's third card is 6 or 7.

Player hand: When first two cards total:

1-2-3-4-5-10	Draws a card
6-7	Stands
8-9	Natural—Stands

Banker hand

First two cards total:	Draws when player's third card is:	Stands when player's third card is:
3	1-2-3-4-5-6-7-9-10	8
4	2-3-4-5-6-7	1-8-9-10
5	4-5-6-7	1-2-3-8-9-10
6	6-7	1-2-3-4-5-8-9-10
7	Stands	
8-0	Natural—Stands	
0-1-2	Always draws	

There are a few exceptions. A natural, as noted above, stops play with no further draws. And if the player has one of its other two standing hands, 6 or 7, bank stands on 6 as well as 7, 8, and 9.

And that's it. Neither hand ever gets more than three cards. After the hands have been played out, the hand totaling closer to 9 wins. Winning bets are paid off at even money. Ties push—neither hand wins nor loses.

Bets on Ties

Bettors also may wager that the two hands will finish with an equal number of points. Winning bets on ties pay off at 8-1. That sounds tempting, but this wager carries a hefty 9.5 percent house edge. Avoid it.

Etiquette

As in other table games, buy chips by placing cash on the layout and asking the dealer for change. The dealer is not allowed to take money directly from players' hands.

If you are the bettor with the largest wager on player and receive the player cards, do not look at them until both player and banker hands have been dealt. And if you hold the banker hand, do not look at the cards until the dealer has flipped the player hand faceup.

Baccarat players are allowed to keep track of the results of each hand, and most casinos provide score sheets and pencils to do so. Most players simply put an X in a column beneath "Banker," "Player," or "Tie."

Strategy

This is a pure guessing game. Which hand will win? The banker hand will win slightly more often—50.68 percent of all decisions, not including ties—giving the house its 1.36 percent edge on player bets. But the house collects a 5 percent commission on winning banker bets, leading to the 1.17 percent house edge on banker.

Mathematicians long have suspected that baccarat, like blackjack, might be vulnerable to a card-counting system. But the best system yet developed appears to yield a slight edge to the bettor on the average of about one hand per eight-deck shoe. That's an edge not worth pursuing—to have the advantage, the customer would have to count down hand after hand after hand, without playing, until this tiny advantage came to pass. The customer would lose more in time than he'd gain in the edge, and the casino would be unlikely to hold a seat for someone spending hours without placing a bet.

For the bettor, baccarat is a game of luck plus money management. Do not make bets too large for your available bankroll, and do not increase bets when losing. Making larger bets while chasing losses is a good way to go broke fast. If you're going to vary your bet size, increase it while winning and bring it down when losing. Set limits on your losses and stick to them.

If you sit down at a mini-baccarat table with $100, tell yourself you're not going to leave with less than $50. Then, if you have a cold streak and you hit that $50 mark, walk away. An important part of casino survival is developing the discipline to leave a table while you still have money.

Learn to walk away with winnings, too. If you have a good run and build that $100 up to $150, try one of these two techniques. Either put the original $100 in your pocket and just play with the $50 in winnings, while keeping that $50 loss limit, or adjust your thinking to tell yourself you'll not walk away from the table with less than $125. Then stick to it.

The longer you play a game with a negative expectation, even one as narrow as 1.17 percent, the more likely it is that the casino will grind down your bankroll. Walk away from the table with at least part of that bankroll intact—not just at baccarat, but at any casino game—and you'll be surprised at how much more often you wind up a winner for the day.

BINGO

Bingo can be as simple as a wire cage with a single caller rotating the handle to make the numbered balls pop out—just the way the game has been played in church basements for generations.

And bingo can be as elaborate as an air blower of the type used in state lotteries, the forced air mixing balls to ensure randomness, while hundreds of players in an enormous hall wait to see if the next ball forced out will complete the pattern displayed on an electronic board.

They're the same game, for at its roots bingo has changed little since Edwin Lowe popularized the name in the 1930s. Lowe, a salesman from New York, didn't invent the game. He discovered it being played at a carnival in Florida under the name "beano," for the dried beans that were being used as markers. After Lowe introduced the game to New York, an excited winner shouted out "bingo!" by mistake, and a name was born.

Today the game is played across the country, with more than 40 states having legalized bingo at some level. The church basement game still thrives, but so do huge bingo halls run by Native American tribes in Arizona, California, Florida, Michigan, Minnesota,

Montana, Nebraska, New Mexico, New York, North Carolina, Oklahoma, Washington, and Wisconsin.

The game has inspired legions of devotees, with "I Love Bingo" shirts, hats, pins with flashing lights, and special pens to mark their cards. For many, the Wednesday night at the American Legion Hall or the weekly trip to the reservation is an event to be anticipated and savored.

At the tribal parlors, prizes can run into thousands of dollars, a far cry from the $20 or $40 games common in games run by churches or service organizations. Many of the full-service tribal casinos that dot the upper Midwest, offering everything from slot machines to blackjack, began as bingo parlors. Even in Nevada, some casinos owe their existence to bingo.

How to Play

Seventy-five balls—15 for each letter in the word bingo—are placed into a wire cage or air blower. Each ball is painted with both a letter and a number; the numbers 1-15 carry the letter B, 16-30 carry letter I, 31-45 are painted with N, 46-60 carry G, and 61-75 are painted with O.

Each player buys at least one card with 25 spaces, arranged with five spaces in each of five vertical columns headed with the letters

B-I-N-G-O. These spaces also make up five horizontal rows. Numbers are printed in 24 spaces; the middle space—third down under N and third across in the middle row—is marked "FREE."

Balls are drawn one at a time, and after each one is drawn, the caller announces the letter and number—"B-3" or "O-65," for example. Players then mark off any spaces on their cards corresponding to the number just announced. In some of the more elaborate setups, players can watch one number being drawn on a big-screen TV while the caller is announcing the previous number. This helps customers playing more than one card to keep up with the game.

A few games still use what are called "hard cards," requiring players to mark numbers with plastic disks or other objects that can be removed. Most games, though, have switched to "throwaways," paper cards that can be marked with a crayon or felt-tip marker and then discarded after each game. Also in use are disposable cards requiring no marker at all— each space has a tab that is folded down after the number is drawn.

When a player has marked off numbers in a pattern that matches the one announced as the winner for that game, the player shouts, "BINGO!" and takes the card to be checked by the caller and an assistant. The assistant can also come to check the card by reading the numbers marked to the caller, who matches them against the list of numbers actually drawn. If the numbers match, the player wins the prize at stake in that game. If more than one player completes a bingo on the same number, the winners split the prize.

Winning Patterns

Most casual players are familiar with the traditional patterns—five in a row, either vertically, horizontally, or diagonally. And these remain the most common patterns, although dozens of patterns are used today. Bingo halls change the patterns being accepted from game to game.

Players must listen to the caller before each new game starts to find out the winning pattern. If the bingo hall has an electronic board in the shape of a bingo card, it will light up spaces corresponding to the shape of that game's pattern. The winning card must have numbers marked in that game's pattern—game personnel will reject a traditional five-in-a-row bingo if the pattern for the game has been announced as a Big Diamond.

Blackout Bingo

A blackout, or coverall, game—frequently involving a large progressive jackpot—has become a staple of many bingo halls. In blackout bingo, the winner must mark off all 25 spaces on the card. If a progressive jackpot

B	I	N	G	O
7	●	42	47	72
14	●	33	59	66
3	●	FREE	52	73
12	●	36	48	68
11	●	43	56	63

VERTICAL

B	I	N	G	O
7	16	42	47	●
14	29	33	●	66
3	24	●	52	73
12	●	36	48	68
●	22	43	56	63

DIAGONAL

B	I	N	G	O
7	16	42	47	72
14	29	33	59	66
3	24	FREE	52	73
●	●	●	●	●
11	22	43	56	63

HORIZONTAL

B	I	N	G	O
●	16	42	47	●
14	●	33	●	66
3	24	●	52	73
12	●	36	●	68
●	22	43	56	●

X MARKS THE SPOT

B	I	N	G	O
●	●	●	●	●
14	29	33	●	66
3	24	●	52	73
12	●	36	48	68
●	22	43	56	63

LUCKY 7

B	I	N	G	O
●	16	42	47	●
14	29	33	59	66
3	24	FREE	52	73
12	18	36	48	68
●	22	43	56	●

4 CORNERS

These patterns show some of the common ways to play bingo.

is involved, the caller will announce how many numbers are to be called. If a 40-number blackout is announced, for example, the first player to mark all 25 numbers called within the 40-number limit wins the progressive jackpot. If no one wins, the jackpot is rolled over until the next night, or next week, or whenever that hall has its next jackpot game.

In some jurisdictions, all prizes must be awarded at the time of play. That effectively rules out a progressive jackpot. In those areas, if a blackout game is announced, numbers must be drawn until there is a winner.

Odds

Unlike other games played in casinos, bingo produces a winner in every game, except for the occasional progressive-jackpot game that features a rollover. So the odds of winning a game are relative to the number of cards in play. If 100 cards are being played in a game, and you are playing two of them, you have two chances in 100, or a 2 percent chance of winning.

That is not the same thing as the house edge we've discussed in other casino games. To get that figure, we need to know what percentage of the bets—in this case, the money spent to buy cards to play—is being returned as prize money. And the answers vary wildly. Some charity games return as little as 50 percent to the players. These games are a low-stress, low-cost way to spend an evening with friends, with an outside chance of winning a few bucks—not a serious gamble. Others, particularly large tribal games with big prizes, sometimes return as much as 80 percent. These are commercial enterprises without the social aspects of the church basement gathering, and they need large returns to keep customers coming back.

Some educated guesses are required by the house—if a $100 game is advertised, that game will pay $100 whether there are ten players or 1,000. But over time, bingo sponsors learn to be close enough in their crowd estimates that the anticipated percentages will hold up.

Whether returning 50 percent, 80 percent, or anything in between, the house has a much larger edge than in other casino games. If the house returns 50 percent of bets as prize money, then the player is bucking a 50 percent house edge. If the house returns 80 percent in prizes, the house edge still is 20 percent. In other games, the largest house edge we've discussed is 16.67 percent on certain proposition bets on the craps table—bets the player should avoid.

But most people don't play bingo as a serious gamble; they play as an evening's entertainment. And for that purpose, bingo has value. A player can stay in action for two or three hours for $10 or $15, an amount that could be gone in three minutes at a $5 blackjack table or a 25-cent slot machine. Even without winning, the player can get caught up in the excitement of being just one number away from that $100 jackpot, without ever putting more than a buck or two at risk at a time.

Playing More than One Card

These days, the player who buys only one card per game is almost a rarity. Bingo fans who think playing multiple cards will improve their chances of winning sometimes buy five, 10, or more cards per game. And players who buy multiple cards will win more games than those who play one card at a time. The problem is, they also will lose more money.

Let's take a perfect series of 100 games, each with a total of 100 cards in use. On the average, over a very long period, each of the 100 cards will win once per 100 games. Now let's say each card costs $1, and the house is returning 80 percent in prize money, so that each game carries an $80 prize.

Player A is playing one card per game, so 100 games will cost $100. On the average, Player A will win one game, for $80 in winnings. Deduct the cost, and Player A has lost $20 over the course of 100 games.

Player B wants to win, and buys 10 cards per game. This player, on the average, will win 10 times for $800 in winnings. But the cards will

HISTORY AND TRIVIA

Bingo's roots are in lotteries, with the Italian National Lottery, established in 1530, regarded as the most likely direct ancestor.

Early in bingo's American history, Edwin Lowe hired Carl Leffler, a professor of mathematics at Columbia University, to develop a series of 6,000 cards without repeating number patterns. Today's cards are based on Leffler's work.

It is estimated that nearly 60 percent of bingo players are women, compared with the figure cited in a 1994 survey that 54 percent of all casino players are women.

have cost $1,000, leaving Player B a net $200 loser.

The disparity gets wider as the house edge increases. If the house is returning only 50 percent in prize money, Player A loses $50 over 100 games and Player B loses $500. If all entries are returned as prizes, both players break even.

Of course, in the real world it is rare that a series of 100 games will work out so perfectly that each of 100 different cards wins once. Things will vary wildly in a short series— Player A might win twice, or three times, or not at all, and Player B might win five times or 15 times in a series as short as 100 trials. But over the long term, results will get closer and closer to the norm.

Playing more than one card at a time gives no mathematical advantage. Does this mean you should never play multiple cards? No, it doesn't. If playing multiple cards enhances your enjoyment of the game, if you can afford the dent in your bankroll, and if you have no trouble keeping track of several cards at once, then by all means, play at your own comfort level. Just don't expect big dividends.

Strategy

Bingo is a game of chance, with no real playing strategy. The best the player can do is to scout out games that offer relatively high paybacks, and perhaps take advantage of a rare night when conditions have kept attendance to lower-than-usual levels. The bingo hall still must award its advertised prizes, and there is less competition to win.

Etiquette

In some halls you buy a card or cards as you walk in; at others, employees or volunteers walk through the crowd, offering cards for sale.

Listen carefully at the beginning of each game to the caller's announcement of that game's winning pattern.

Don't play more cards than you can comfortably track at one time.

KENO

Like bingo, keno is lottery-derived, but the two games are a continent apart. Keno's roots are in China, and the game was brought to the United States by Chinese immigrants in the late 1800s. It was originally played with 80 Chinese characters, which in the United States were replaced by 80 Arabic numerals.

For a time in Nevada, each number was accompanied by the name of a racehorse, and the game was known as racehorse keno. The horses' names disappeared in 1951, when a tax on off-track betting on horses was passed. Operators didn't want their game mistaken as betting on the horses. Still, remnants of racehorse keno games remain. Many casinos still call each game a "race"—if you bet on more than one game at once, you buy a multirace ticket.

Almost all Nevada casinos have keno lounges, where numbered balls are forced out through an air blower to determine the winners. Some tribal casinos in the upper Midwest also have live keno lounges, and Atlantic City began offering live keno in 1994. On riverboat casinos, keno players settle for a video version, which offers less flexibility of play than live keno but usually has a better percentage pay table.

How to Play

In the live version, the player may mark anywhere from 1 through 20 numbers on a card that has 80 numbers arranged in eight rows of ten. The player then takes the card to a keno writer and places a bet that the numbers selected will be among the 20 drawn in the next game. Alternatively, the player sitting in one of the casino restaurants can mark a card and give it with a bet to a keno runner, who takes it to the keno writer and then brings back the ticket. The bet is in multiples of the house minimum—usually $1 nowadays, though 70-cent games still are fairly common at smaller Nevada casinos.

After the 20 numbers are drawn, winning tickets are paid according to a table that varies from house to house. For example, a four-spot ticket with $1 wagered might return the $1 if two numbers hit, bring $5 if three numbers hit, and pay $120 if all four come in. But in another casino, the three-number hit might pay $6 and all four $125, and in another the payoffs might be $5 and $110. Because of the variation, no payback percentage is common enough to be called average. Paybacks range from below 70 percent to more than 80 percent.

Bets

Straight ticket: Betting the numbers marked as a single wager is called betting a straight ticket. It's the simplest way to play, but many players like to bet more combinations. One popular method is the "way ticket." For example, a player might mark six numbers, circle two groups of three, and mark on the side of the ticket, "2/3, 1/6." The player then would bet $3 to have $1 wagers on each of two three-spot combinations and on the six-spot.

King ticket: A number circled by itself is the king, which is used in all combinations marked. Let's say a seventh number in the

KENO					ACCOUNT NO.		PRICE PER GAME	
MARK NUMBER OF SPOTS OR WAYS PLAYED					NO. OF GAMES		TOTAL PRICE	

1	2	3	4	5	6	7	8	9	10
11	12	13	14	15	16	17	18	19	20
21	22	23	24	25	26	27	28	29	30
31	32	33	34	35	36	37	38	39	40
41	42	43	44	45	46	47	48	49	50
51	52	53	54	55	56	57	58	59	60
61	62	63	64	65	66	67	68	69	70
71	72	73	74	75	76	77	78	79	80

A typical keno ticket.

previous example was circled as a king. The
player then could mark "2/4, 1/7" to bet two
four-number combinations—the king joining
each of the three-number groupings—and the
overall seven numbers.

Combination ticket: The player marks
several number groupings and plays
combinations of them. For example, a ticket
with two-, three-, and four-number groupings
can be played as 1/2, 1/3, 1/4, 1/5 (the two- and
three-number groups together), 1/6 (two- and
four-number groups), 1/7 (three- and four-
numbers), 1/9 (all three groups). At $1 per
game, the ticket would cost $7.

Progressive Jackpots

For higher-number totals played, or for bigger
bets, many keno games offer progressive
jackpots. Sometimes the progressive jackpot
gets high enough that the house is actually
offering more than 100 percent payback. Late
in 1994, the jackpot on a $2 eight-spot ticket
surpassed $200,000 at a casino in Las Vegas.
At the $250,000 jackpot cap, the player would
have an edge of 17.4 percent. Now that doesn't
mean a player could sit down and win steadily
at a 17 percent rate. Results can vary wildly
over a short period of time. A player can expect
to hit eight-of-eight on the average of once
every 230,000 trials, and the casino's eight-spot
was paying nothing below five-of-eight spots,
so only 2 percent of all tickets would collect
anything at all.

Strategy

Overall, the returns at keno are too infrequent for anyone to play the game seriously. A game or two over breakfast in the casino coffee shop or relaxing in the keno lounge is plenty for many people. But some players on a tight budget enjoy sitting in the keno lounge, being served free drinks and playing a buck at a time as an inexpensive way to spend the day.

For someone who wants to play seriously enough to go from casino to casino, the best strategy is simply to compare pay tables and play at the house that pays the most for the number of spots you select. There is no strategy for selecting numbers—any number is as likely to come up as any of the others.

Video Keno

Video keno is essentially the same game—the same 80 numbers arranged in the same eight rows on a video screen. There are no way tickets, or kings, or combinations. The player touches the screen with an electronic pen, and the numbers marked are played as a straight ticket. Pay tables are better than at live keno.

Keno machines are most frequently available at the 25-cent level, though there are some five-cent machines and a few $1 machines. Because no keno writers or runners are needed and no lines of players are waiting for their tickets, video keno plays much faster than the live game.

OTHER CASINO GAMES

The most common games offered in American casinos are the enduring favorites. However, new games of chance are being developed all the time, and a few older games hold a limited amount of casino floor space. Here's a look at some other games you may encounter in the United States.

Caribbean Stud Poker

A favorite at Caribbean casinos and on cruise ships in the 1980s, this variation on five-card stud poker rapidly carved out a niche in Nevada in the early '90s. It has spread to casinos in the South, the Midwest, and Atlantic City so widely that soon more Caribbean Stud tables may be in operation than roulette wheels or baccarat/mini-baccarat tables.

The game was designed to appeal to those players who possess more experience at slot machines or video poker than at other table games. All winning bets are paid off according to a pay table similar to video poker's, and most tables have a large progressive jackpot for a royal flush.

Caribbean Stud is played at a seven-player, blackjack-sized table. In front of each player are areas marked "Ante" and "Bet," and most tables also have a slot into which the player slides a chip if he wishes to take a chance on the progressive jackpot.

Play begins with each player placing a chip or chips in the ante area. Each player and the dealer then receive five cards dealt from a single 52-card deck. All player cards are dealt facedown, and one dealer card is turned faceup. Players then may look at their cards, picking them up with one hand. If you think your hand can beat the dealer's, you place a bet of exactly double the amount of the ante and place your cards facedown next to the ante. If you don't think your hand can win, you fold by putting the cards down in front of your betting area without making a bet. The house then takes the ante.

Hand	Payoff
Pair or less	1-1
Two pair	2-1
Three of a kind	3-1
Straight	4-1
Flush	5-1
Full house	7-1
Four of a kind	20-1
Straight flush	50-1
Royal flush	100-1

After all players have either bet or folded, the dealer's cards are turned faceup. The dealer's hand is a qualifying hand if it consists of ace-king or better. The house takes the bets and antes of any hands that do not beat the dealer. On hands that beat the dealer's qualifying hand, the ante is paid off at 1-1, and bets are paid according to the pay table.

If the dealer's hand is not at least ace-king, it does not qualify. Antes are paid off at 1-1, but bets are off—regardless of the player's hand.

For example, the player antes $5, sees his hand consists of a pair of 8s and a pair of 6s, and makes a $10 bet. The dealer has a pair of 10s—a qualifying hand—so the player wins $5 on the ante and $20 on the 2-1 payoff on the bet. If the dealer's hand did not qualify—10 as the high card with no pairs, for example—the player would win $5 on the ante, but no money would change hands on the bet. And if the dealer had another pair to go with the pair of 10s, his two pair would outrank the player's two pair and the house would take both the ante and bet.

The house edge is about 5.6 percent—pretty high by table games standards. The attraction, in addition to jackpot possibilities, is the game's leisurely pace and its ease of play. Strategy is simple—bet any time you have a pair or better, or if you have ace-king and another card that matches the dealer's faceup card. For example, if the dealer's faceup card is a 6, you would play ace-king-7-6-3 but discard ace-king-8-7-3. That may seem odd, because ace-king-8-7-3 outranks ace-king-7-6-3. But since you have a 6 to match the dealer's up-card, the dealer is less likely to have a pair to beat your ace-king. This advantage is just enough to make the hand playable.

The progressive jackpot requires a separate bet, usually $1. Pay tables vary from casino to casino, but most offer flat amounts for a flush, full house, or four of a kind—either 10 percent of the jackpot or a flat amount for a straight flush, and the full jackpot for a royal flush. At most casinos, after a royal flush is hit, the progressive jackpot begins anew at $5,000 or $10,000. When the jackpot meter is at its rollover value, the house edge exceeds 20 percent. The break-even point, with no house edge, is past $200,000.

The percentage player can find better bets in the casino. But with its blend of relaxed play with jackpot possibilities, Caribbean Stud seems on its way to becoming a casino staple.

Let it Ride

Another variation on five-card stud poker, Let It Ride made its first appearance in casinos in 1994. From the initial reaction in its test market of Nevada, the game appears to have the potential to sweep the nation once it has approval from individual state gaming boards.

Let It Ride has many of the same strengths of Caribbean Stud poker. It takes advantage of the easy familiarity many Americans have with poker hands and has a pay table like video poker's. It does not feature a large progressive jackpot as Caribbean Stud does, but it has a lower house edge on the basic bet— about 2.8 percent. And the player faces less potential risk in Let It Ride. A Caribbean Stud player at a $5 table faces a loss of $15 on a $5 ante and $10 bet if the dealer's hand beats the player's. The $5 Let It Ride player, on the other hand, starts with $15 on the table in three $5 bets but has the option of pulling back two of the bets if the cards aren't favorable, leaving a real risk of $5 a hand.

There is no dealer hand to beat; all payoffs are according to the pay table, with the minimum winning hand being a pair of 10s or better.

The game is played at a blackjack-sized, seven-player table. Each player has three betting circles on the layout and must make three equal bets to begin play. The dealer gives each player three cards facedown from a single 52-card deck, then two more cards are placed facedown in front of the dealer. Those two cards are common to all hands—the player makes a five-card poker hand by using his own three cards plus the two in front of the dealer.

After all cards are dealt, the player looks at his three cards and decides whether to let all three

bets ride or whether to pull back the first bet.
To let it ride, the player slides his cards under
the first chip; to pull back the first bet, he
scratches the table with his cards, and the
dealer then pushes the chips in the betting
circle back to the player.

The dealer then turns the first common card
faceup. The player may either let the second
bet ride or pull it back. The third bet must
stand—it may not be pulled back—and players
slide their cards facedown under their chips
before the final card is turned faceup.

The dealer then turns each player's cards
faceup in turn and settles all bets.

Hand	Payoff
Pair of 10s or better	1-1
Two pair	2-1
Three of a kind	3-1
Straight	5-1
Flush	8-1
Full house	11-1
Four of a kind	50-1
Straight flush	200-1

Most strategy is obvious: After three cards, Let
It Ride if you have a pair of 10s or better, pull
back the bets if you don't. After the fourth, also

Let It Ride if you have four parts of a flush. Don't chase four-card straights.

Pai-Gow Poker

An Americanized version of the Chinese game of pai-gow, which is played with dominoes, pai-gow poker is most common in Nevada, Atlantic City, and on some riverboats in Mississippi. Though pai-gow poker has a following, it moves too slowly to make it profitable enough to earn its keep on the space-limited riverboats of the Midwest.

Pai-gow poker is dealt from a 53-card deck— the standard 52 cards plus a joker, which may be used as an ace or to complete straights or flushes. It is the one fairly common game in American casinos in which a player may act as the banker, covering other players' bets and paying the house a commission on wagers won by the bank. However, many casinos restrict how often the player may act as the banker, and many players choose not to act as banker, so players frequently play against the dealer.

Each player is dealt seven cards, which he must arrange into a five-card—or high—hand and a two-card—or second high—hand. Cards must be arranged so that the five-card hand outranks the two-card hand, or the player automatically loses. For example, if the seven cards include a pair of kings and a pair of 6s, the player may not place the pair of kings in the two-card hand.

The highest-ranking two-card hand is a pair of aces—there are no straights or flushes in two cards. The five-card hand is ranked according to normal poker hands. For the player to win, he must beat both the dealer's five-card and two-card hands—or the banker's if a player is holding the bank. The dealer/banker wins if he wins both hands. If the player wins one hand and the dealer/banker wins the other, the hand is a push and no money changes hands.

All winning hands, whether player hands or by a player acting as the banker, pay the house a commission—usually 5 percent. In addition, the dealer/banker hand has a slight edge over the players, because any identical hands, called copy hands, are won by the dealer/ banker. This happens most frequently on the two-card hand. The dealer/banker still must win the five-card hand to take the bet.

Because of the copy-hand rule, a player acting as banker plays at a slightly lower disadvantage to the house than the other players. However, the banker faces a higher risk, because he must cover the bets of all the other players. Do not attempt to act as the banker with a short bankroll.

No easy, quick strategy exists for setting hands in pai-gow poker. Beginners should attempt to make the two-card hand as strong as possible while staying within the rule that the five-card hand must outrank the two-card hand. For example, in a hand with no pairs, place the highest card in the five-card hand and the next two highest in the two-card hand. With one pair, place it in the five-card hand, while taking the two highest of the remaining cards for the two-card hand. If you have two pair, most often you'll place the high pair in the five-card hand and the low pair in the two-card hand. However, if you hold an ace or king in addition to the two pair, leave the two pair together in the five-card hand and place the ace or king in the two-card hand.

Setting the cards takes time, and many hands result in pushes as the player wins one portion and the dealer/banker wins the other. This produces too few decisions per hour for casinos with space limitations.

Multiple-Action Blackjack

Play is much the same as regular blackjack, except that each player has three betting circles and the dealer has three rectangles in front of him. The player must make at least two bets at a time, and most players make three.

Each player receives two cards, just as in regular blackjack, but the dealer receives only an up-card, placed in the first rectangle, before players make hit/stand decisions. Any player who busts loses the wagers in all three betting circles. For those remaining, the dealer now plays the original up-card in three separate hands, one to settle bets in each circle.

After all player hands have been completed, the dealer gets a second card, then makes all hit/stand decisions as normal—hitting 16 and less, standing on 17 or more. When the dealer either stands or busts, he uses the result to settle all bets in the first betting circle. He then moves the original up-card to the second rectangle and plays the hand out to settle bets in the second circle. Finally, he moves the same up-card to the third rectangle and plays yet again to settle bets in the third circle.

The percentages are exactly the same as in regular blackjack. Many players try to limit their losses by standing on hands they should hit in hopes that the dealer will bust one of the three hands. This is a mistake. The dealer still will make 17 or better with a 10 showing more than 80 percent of the time, just as in regular blackjack. The player's best chance, in the long run, is to follow the same basic strategy detailed in the blackjack section.

Yes, it is difficult for a $5 player to see three $5 bets wiped out at once when the player busts. But playing a never-bust strategy increases the house edge from less than 1 percent to about 5 percent. If you cannot stand to see three bets lose on one turn of the card, don't play multiple action.

Big Six Wheel

The big six, or money, wheel is simply a variation on the old carnival wheel of fortune.

It was a lousy play at the carnival, and it's a lousy play at the casino.

The wheel stands upright and is divided into nine sections, each of which has spaces for six symbols. Fifty-two of the symbols consist of U.S. currency—24 $1 bills, 15 $2 bills, seven $5 bills, four $10 bills, and two $20 bills. The other two spaces usually go to a casino logo and either a joker or an American eagle.

A dealer stands in front of the wheel, keeps track of bets, and spins the wheel. In front of the dealer is a layout with each currency unit plus each special symbol. Players bet by placing a chip or chips on the symbol of their choice. The symbol on which the wheel stops is the winner. Bets on $1 pay even money, bets on $2 pay 2-1, bets on $5 pay 5-1, bets on $10 pay 10-1, bets on $20 pay 20-1, and bets on the special symbols each pay 40-1.

The house advantage is enormous—11.1 percent on $1, 16.6 percent on $2, 22.2 percent on $5, 18.5 percent on $10, 22.2 percent on $20, and 24 percent on either special symbol. Look at it this way: If you were to bet a dollar on the $1 symbol a perfect series of 54 spins in which each space came up once, you would win 24 times and lose 30. At the end of the series you would have $48 left of the $54 you wagered. The house would have won a net of $6 in the sequence— 6/54 of your wagers, or 11.1 percent. And that's the best bet of the bunch.